MEMO FROM
RUSSIA

MEMO FROM RUSSIA

By
Stan Rose
Photography and Special Editing
By
Shirley Rose

THE LOWELL PRESS/KANSAS CITY
1986

Cover design by Dorothy Day
Editing assistance by Katie Ingels Gusewelle
FIRST EDITION
Copyright © 1986 by Stan Rose
All rights reserved
Library of Congress Cataloging-in-Publications Data
Rose, Stan.
Memo from Russia.
1. Soviet Union—Description and travel—1970-
2. Rose, Stan, 1918-   . I. Rose, Shirley, 1921-
II. Title.
DK29.R664 1986   914.7'0485   86-2780
ISBN 0-932845-13-4 (soft: alk. paper)

This book was photocomposed in Palatino and
printed on Warren's Olde Style,
a neutral pH paper with an expected 300-year
library storage life as determined by the
Council of Library Resources of the
American Library Association,
by The Lowell Press, Inc., of Kansas City, Missouri.

To my Boss Lady, Shirley,
who has blue-pencilled almost every
column I have written in
more than 35 years, and to my children,
grandchildren, and Mom and Pop, who have let
me share this wonderful woman
and take her to faraway places.

ACKNOWLEDGMENT

Some of the chapters first appeared in the *Sun Newspapers*. I am grateful to Irl Krause, *Sun* production manager, and his fine staff for technical assistance.

TABLE OF CONTENTS

Foreword xi
Introduction xiii
    Impressions 1

Chapter

1	System the Culprit in Shallow Reporting . . .	5
2	Will the Soviets Ever Look Us in the Eye? . . .	8
3	In the Land of Nyets	11
4	It Takes More Than One City to Know Russia . .	15
5	A Professor Helps Solve a Mystery	20
6	First News Story Gave Us a Bad Moment . . .	23
7	Russian "Prizes" Beat the Pulitzer	26
8	The Unions Take Over as Proxy Parents	29
9	Goose-Stepping Soldiers—A Powerful Reminder .	38
10	Pectopah—The McDonald's of Russia?	47
11	Chet Gives Us a Hot Scoop on Afghanistan . . .	50
12	Inflexible Rules Win Out in the End	54
13	Stores Excel in Organized Inefficiency	57
14	Rules or Not, Tipping Is a Way of Life	61
15	The Icebreaker Strikes Again	64
16	Gorbachev Gives Them Something to Look Forward to—2 P.M.	70

17	A Miracle Lenin Had No Part Of	73
18	Black Market Hack Gets a Ransom for a Ride	76
19	"Twelve Years Is Long Enough to Wait..."	80
20	If Bears Can Play Ice Hockey...	85
	Faces and Places	87
21	If I Could Have Erased Nadia's Fears	95
22	Beware of Friendship Tours	98
23	Everyone But the Public Has a Right to Know	101
24	Dr. Volchenko Raps Open-Heart Surgery	105
25	Kids Take Our Words with a Grain of Salt	109
26	Soviet Customs Inspectors Master Art of Harassment	112
27	Independent Spirits Abound in Siberia	116
28	A Surprising Crowd at Kiev's Synagogue	118
29	How Long Before Nobody Comes?	123
30	This Region Needs a Name Change	127
31	Show Biz on the Trans-Siberian Railroad	131
32	Russia Didn't Scare Me, Thanks to Max	137
33	Comforting Thoughts on Chances for Peace	140
34	A Tribute to Russia's Ice Cream	143
35	Alexi Is at a Loss for Words	145
36	How We Finally Got Our Coffee *with* Breakfast	148
37	Now...a Few Words from Gorbachev	151
38	Where Could They Send Us—Siberia?	155
39	Racing Thoughts on the Bullet Train	159

FOREWORD

STAN ROSE, my father, is one of those rare individuals who has been blessed with a "third eye."

A hundred people may travel to the same spots and visually see the same things, but the one with the special insight, the "third eye," is able to come away with a better understanding of what is really going on beyond what most of us see.

The most common comment one hears about the many columns Stan Rose has written from his worldwide travels is, "I've never read that before."

Stan Rose has the unique ability to discern a mosaic from his travels, blending together the political, economic and man-in-the-street picture of a nation.

The latest of his worldwide trips is the most significant. Russia, more than any other, seems to have been the enigma waiting for his special eye.

More than the trips to China, Eastern Europe, South Africa, India, Western Europe, or South America, the Soviet Union journey was like peeking at the dark side of the moon.

Most who have visited this mysterious nation have been

restricted from any really free experience to visit its people.

Somehow, my father and mother, Shirley, managed to escape much of the trite tourist program, to interview, to film and to write about the people of the Soviet Union.

Readers of the *Sun Newspapers* and now the readers of this book are fortunate.

An unusually free-wheeling trip through the Soviet Union by individuals who can capture the multifaceted landscape is a real treat and, perhaps, a once in a lifetime opportunity for a special look at Russia through a man's "three" eyes.

STEVE ROSE, President
Sun Publications

INTRODUCTION

THE U.S. National Newspaper Association representative who had been trying for months to finalize details of our pending 1985 trip to the Soviet Union was never quite certain from one day to the next whether our project was on or off.

The patient newspaperwoman would keep us posted on the latest developments, and our plans remained in limbo for months while we waited for an indecisive Soviet Embassy in Washington to reach a final decision.

When the happy news arrived late last summer that all signals were go, we made preparations for a September 26 departure from Kennedy International Airport to Leningrad, with a stopover in Helsinki, Finland.

Twenty-three members of the Association would be taking off together on the Finnair 747 jet, but six had signed up for only a portion of the month-long trip. They would leave the group in Central Asia. The remaining seventeen would continue through Siberia and Mongolia, with our trip culminating in a 2,500-mile train ride to the Russian Far East Territory on the Trans-Siberian Railroad. We would end our "round-the-world" adventure with a stopover in Japan.

Naturally, the opinions expressed in this book are strictly my own, and I hold none of those witty and charming traveling companions responsible in any way for my often critical views. I hope, in turn, they don't hold me responsible for theirs.

Stan Rose

STAN ROSE

Kansas City, March, 1986

xiv MEMO FROM RUSSIA

OUR TRAVEL ROUTE

Introduction

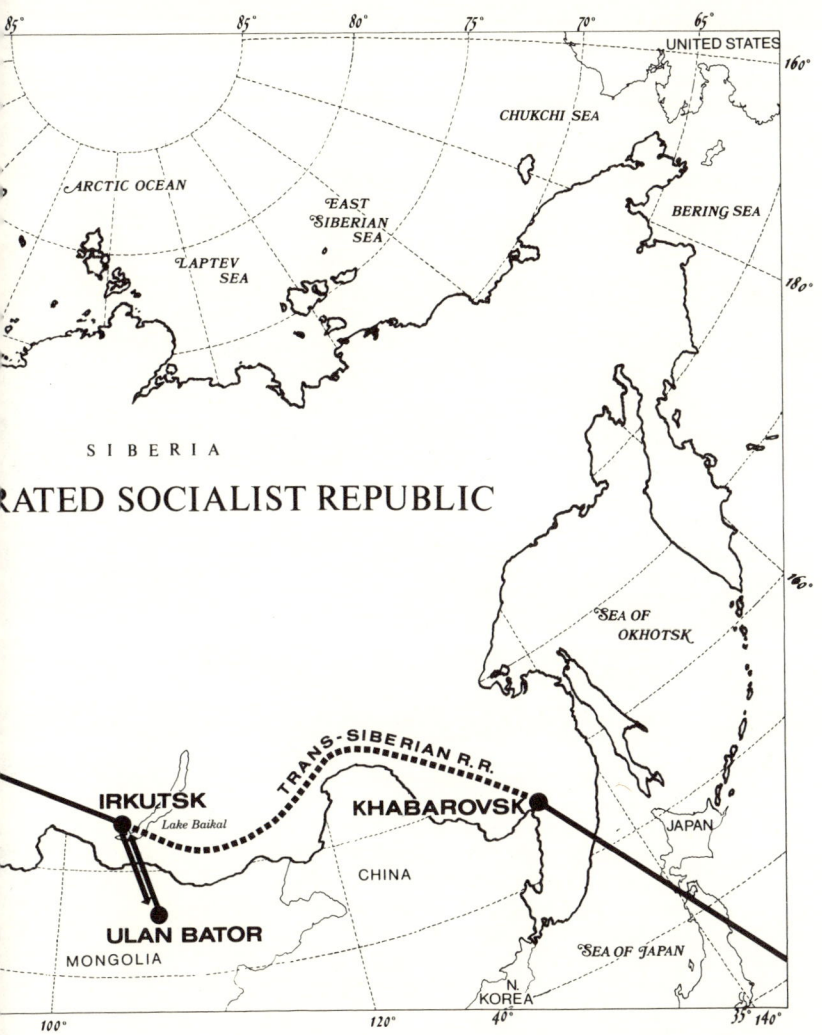

The route of the author's 10,000-mile, month-long journey across the vastness of the Soviet Union, from Helsinki, Finland, on the Baltic Sea, south and eastward through 11 time zones to Khabarovsk near the Sea of Japan.

IMPRESSIONS

REMEMBERING SOME OF THE GOOD MOMENTS

THERE WERE TIMES when we almost fell in love with Russia. The big, clumsy, backward country reaches out and touches your heart just when you've given up.

There were times one could forget the stifling bureaucracy, the rude clerks and pompous officials who must take correspondence courses in harassment, and the stinking public toilets that foul the air from Moscow to the faraway Pacific.

On the rare occasions when a tourist could get close to the people and penetrate the barrier of reserve and supervision fostered by an unceasing barrage of propaganda, wonderful things happened. . . .

A little boy laughs at the clowns at the great Russian circus, and for a fleeting moment our eyes meet those of his proud parents and we share, the four of us, the meaning of love.

A middle-aged woman, treasuring the Polaroid picture Shirley has just given her, suddenly embraces her and plants a big kiss on Shirley's cheek. "America!" Shirley shouts proudly, tapping her own chest.

"America!" the woman echoes approvingly. Soon we are surrounded by curious, smiling passersby on the promenade that Sunday morning in Irkutsk, Siberia. And in response to several other requests, Shirley keeps her Polaroid clicking. What an icebreaker and Nyet-stopper that Polaroid is! One hundred pictures and Shirley keeps none for herself. At times, the Russians shower us with flowers and gifts in return.

A waiter on the Trans-Siberian Railroad suddenly transforms himself into an accomplished musician one evening after dinner and the communication gap between us is broken by the international language: music. A heavy-set cleaning woman suddenly turns into a prima ballerina — almost — and dances lightly across the dining car floor to the Russian melodies.

The waiter is playing a small accordion, which Alexi, one of our national guides, insists on calling a harmonica. Alexi has taught us a Russian song and by the second night on the train we are able to carry it off fairly well.

The dining car and those precious evenings belong exclusively to us — American newspaper people — because the bureaucracy isolates us from the Russian passengers. . . .

The ice hockey game where our guide leads us as we root for the home team, Novosibirsk, and where the crowd of about 8,000 in the modern arena is enthusiastic but restrained. Most Russians, as we observe, are heavy smokers and heavy drinkers, but have no trouble adapting to the rules at Russian sports events: no smoking and no drinking.

The game ends in a tie. Russian ice hockey as we watch it played there is a sissy's version of American mayhem on the rink. I'll take mine Russian style. . . .

The basketball game where classical music is played during halftime while substitutes on the team shoot baskets. We cheer for the home team, and it drubs the opposition. The giants from the visiting team are staying at our hotel and we learn through interpreters that they all work for a factory in another Siberian town. Their jobs? Playing basketball, of course. Their sponsor is the factory's trade union. Every factory has a trade union, which handles every aspect of a member's life. The trade union is an arm of the Soviet government and membership is compulsory. . . .

And the moment when our guide Alexi fights back the tears as our group gives him a farewell party on the night before our departure from Russia.

Alexi's earlier hostility is no longer evident as we drink a toast to his health — "na zdorovie" — and present him with a gift. This is all too much. "We wish you peace," we assure him and hope that for that moment, at least, he believes us.

CHAPTER 1

SYSTEM THE CULPRIT IN SHALLOW REPORTING

AMONG THE COMMENTS we've most often heard since we began writing, talking and showing our TV films, this one stands out:

"You've shown us a side of Russia we haven't seen before."

We take that as a compliment, of course, but let's be honest. Anyone in the American media working for a living as a correspondent in Moscow would be booted out of Russia on his ear if he tried to tell it as I am telling it now.

The shallow, so-called objective American reporting that comes from Moscow in our daily papers, newsmagazines and TV is a strategy of self-preservation. In the most closely regimented society we've seen anywhere in the world, including the Iron Curtain countries and China, foreign journalists are as much prisoners of the political system as are the 280 million citizens of the Soviet Union.

Add to the timid acceptance of their lot the fact that 30 American correspondents in Moscow have to live in special compounds for foreigners and we realize that ignorance as well as expediency plays a part in the poor quality of reporting.

Their isolation by the Soviet Government gives them little or no chance to get to know the average Soviet citizen. As the Moscow Bureau Chief for Associated Press told us in a rare moment of candor:

"We could live here a long, long time and never know the place. The Soviet citizen is aware that he has too much to lose if he shows the slightest inclination to become friendly. He is by nature suspicious of foreigners and is made additionally suspicious of foreign journalists.

"I assume that everything said here is being heard," bureau chief Roxinne Ervasti continued defiantly. "We are always under surveillance."

Who's reporting on the reporters?

It was almost funny to hear the AP representative tell it. "There's always a babushka (female state supervisor-attendant, usually fat, middle-aged or elderly) in the hall when I come home to my apartment in the evening." She didn't have to say more. We'd seen babushkas sweeping the streets. We'd seen them — as key ladies on every floor of our hotels — plainly dressed, sometimes smiling but usually not, and nearly always suspiciously hostile.

With our group of American publishers it was different. We were on a once-in-a-lifetime trip. No one was concerned about losing a job or even about getting an early departure for home. Those who wanted to comply with the structured itinerary went to the museums. Some of us dared from the very beginning to go off on our own and adventure. . . .

I haven't checked with the intelligent, well-traveled folks who shared our experience in the world's largest country, but I'll bet we independently came to the same conclusion.

The nonsense that we must avoid the truth so that we don't risk angering the bullying, blustering, self-serving

System the Culprit in Shallow Reporting 7

aristocrats in the Kremlin must stop. If we can help stop it, we'll have done a good deed for all mankind, even at the risk — not of nuclear war, of course — but of the cancelling of future trips by Russia.

Ironically, we feel better now about the chances of seeing a significant slowing of the arms race and avoiding the risks of accidental war than we did before we went to the Soviet Union. Seeing with our own eyes the monumental task that Mikhail Gorbachev has before him — the task of bringing the Soviet Union into the 20th century as we prepare to enter the 21st — we are somewhat comforted. His dedication to getting his country moving after 68 years of dismal post-revolution failure is commendable.

If Gorbachev is to make good on so much as part of the promises he has made, he will have to shift the focus of Soviet policies from nuclear missiles and nuclear submarines to making a stagnant economy work. He will have to give the Russian people a reason to live besides slogans, inspirational pep talks and vodka.

And, as Gorbachev knows far better than we who spent only a month in his country, he can't get much more mileage out of the fable that America is going to attack the Soviet Union.

Beneath the average Russian's suspicious, unfriendly, and sometimes rude exterior sometimes lies a warmth toward America that seems to reject the baloney coming out of the Kremlin.

We know. We broke the ice with a Polaroid camera and a TV camera and have the evidence to prove that the camera never lies.

CHAPTER 2

WILL THE SOVIETS EVER LOOK US IN THE EYE?

A MONTH-LONG VISIT to the Soviet Union, crossing 11 time zones within its borders, doesn't make us experts on that huge, complicated nation. But having had the previous benefit of traveling to almost 100 countries on five continents, including several Iron Curtain countries, we can say this:

There is only one Soviet Union. No country begins to match it when it comes to the relentless drip, drip, drip of internal propaganda and programming that emanates from the Kremlin to every one of the 15 so-called Autonomous Republics and Autonomous Regions within the borders of the biggest country on earth. Autonomous, my eye. What a joke!

The Wonderful Wizard of Oz, that loveable fraud unmasked by Dorothy (Judy Garland) in Hollywood's 1939 film version of Frank Baum's famous book, controlled his mythical empire by scaring his citizens half to death. The Wiz was a piker compared to the Kremlin bosses, past and present — bosses hand-picked by the

Will the Soviets Ever Look Us in the Eye?

ruling regime of the Communist Party whose rigid admittance rules require a lifetime of total dedication and achievement.

Only seven percent of the Soviet Union qualify for membership in The Party. That's seven percent of 280 million. So according to my pocket calculator, which may not be quite as dependable as the abacus still used exclusively in virtually every store and kiosk in the world's No. 2 superpower (computers? what are computers?), fewer than 20 million individuals hold absolute rein over the other 260 million.

And although the newest Boss Man, Mikhail Gorbachev, may be more enlightened than his predecessors, he is not about to loosen that rein to any great extent.

Chances are that somebody — maybe one of the deputy directors we met at the Soviet Ministry of Foreign Affairs — will be shown these reports written after our return from the USSR. If he comments, his response will undoubtedly be, "The man came here hating us. What do you expect?"

Nuts. We went to the Soviet Union, Shirley and I, determined to see and enjoy the experience of our lives. Those TV spy thrillers and paperback novels like *Gorky Park* were figments of fertile, creative minds back home.

Sure enough, Gorky Park looked more peaceful than Central Park and probably was safer to walk by night. We never identified a KGB agent lurking behind any bushes or lampposts when we went off on our own, and if our room was "bugged" by anything more menacing than a few little crawly things, we never uncovered the wires.

It was the stifling bureaucracy that finally wore us down. A rigid schedule of morning to night activities and meetings was designed to exclude the one thing we wanted to see most in the Soviet Union — the Soviet people. Not the bureaucrats, but the people. After tolerating that schedule a while, we began to leave our group and go off on our own.

The bureaucrats, with their defenses always up despite their halfhearted efforts to be charming, at least provided us with a dialogue. The people were unapproachable, except for a few we met by chance and by design and by Polaroid. The people of the Soviet Union do not make eye contact. There is no way of transmitting human warmth to someone who is literally afraid to talk to a stranger. There was no special objection because we were American. The distrust is aimed at all strangers and at each other.

Whether Mikhail Gorbachev will move even a little bit closer in the direction of trusting strangers and, more importantly, trusting the Soviet people is doubted in the American Embassy in Moscow, but anything can happen. I hazard a guess that Gorbachev is on the spot and that something surprisingly constructive will come out of his summit meetings with President Reagan.

If Gorbachev fails to get the Soviet Union moving, it will sooner or later revert to the rule of the old men again and to the paralysis that made a dismal failure of 11 five-year plans.

CHAPTER 3

IN THE LAND OF NYETS

THERE IS NO RIGHT WAY to start describing the hectic, tiring, frustrating, but unforgettable, experience we wouldn't have missed for the world and wouldn't repeat for all the tea in China and the Soviet Union put together.

On the whole, I think Russian tea is better, but it was more fun drinking tea in China back in 1980, because we were treated as welcome guests in that communist country. In Russia, which should correctly be called the Union of Soviet Socialist Republics because Russia is just one of the 15 dissimilar Soviet republics that makes up the physical entity known as the world's largest nation, we were . . . well, I guess, tolerated is the word.

The elite Communist Party bureaucrats in the Kremlin, who insist on spoon-feeding and thought-controlling every living, breathing one of the nation's 280 million residents, have a capacity for messing up almost everything including good intentions.

Our first brush with the stifling tyranny that emanates from the awesome Red Square came at our Intourist hotel on Gorky Street in Moscow, just across from the Kremlin. We'd been told in Leningrad that someone in the English-

A leisurely afternoon at Red Square.

In the Land of Nyets

speaking Service Bureau at our Moscow hotel would surely help us find a place to get the battery charger for our video camera repaired.

It had burned out the first time we plugged it into the wall socket. We'd used the proper converter and plug, but the sensitive charger couldn't stand the current. The video camera was my right arm. We were desperate. At the Service Bureau we got one snippy "Nyet" after another from the English-speaking personnel. *Nyet* is the national byword which means almost everything from just plain "No!" to "Don't bug me, I'm on coffee break." These breaks seem to occur at least 20 times a day in tourist-related facilities, and when they do, everything shuts down. *Nyet* also means "finished," which is a time-worn way of saying, "We don't have anymore of whatever it is you want to buy."

Charming, pretty Olga, an English-speaking clerk at the front desk, responded with sympathy to our problem. She was like a breath of fresh air. "I will send for an electrician. He will come to the hotel and fix your battery charger." She spoke with soothing assurance. An electrician came. He couldn't fix the charger but managed to recharge the dead batteries. We were ready for action, with the video camera.

Next morning, we needed the electrician again, but Olga was off for the day. Employees at the hotels work long hours but only on alternate days. Her replacement, a cold, middle-aged woman, listened to our plea for help. "We don't provide that service," she snapped. We weren't about to be turned away. We persisted and she seemingly made a phone call. "Go to your room and wait," she commanded. "If someone can do anything for you, we'll call you."

We made the mistake of telling the woman about Olga just to convince her the whole thing wasn't such a big deal. She didn't bat an eye. "Go to your room and wait," she repeated. We went to our room and waited until we finally realized nobody would come.

The next day, we found sweet Olga at her station. Before we could finish telling her our problem, she interrupted, "I'm sorry but I cannot provide you with that service again." Her voice was mechanical. On prompting, she admitted, "The woman who took my place yesterday reported me for helping you. I am truly sorry, but I can't afford to get into trouble again."

We said we understood. To our astonishment, Olga hesitated a moment and then said defiantly, "I hope you can find a camera store to solve your problem. If you cannot, come back to the desk tonight, and I will find a way to help you."

We didn't know it then, but Olga's spark of independence was one of the few examples of free thinking we would witness in our 10,000-mile travels from the tourist cities of Leningrad and Moscow to southern Russia and across Siberia via the Trans-Siberian Railroad.

CHAPTER 4

IT TAKES MORE THAN ONE CITY TO KNOW RUSSIA

LENINGRAD may be Russia's second largest city, but it's certainly first in beauty. Russia's giant state-run tourist agency, Intourist, couldn't have planned a more impressive first stop for travelers visiting the Soviet Union. We were among the lucky ones.

Coming in by plane from Helsinki, as we did, or by ship to the famed Baltic Sea port of Leningrad, tourists are bound to get a thrilling first impression. The 18th century baroque architecture, inspired and created by Peter the Great, founder in 1703 of Saint Petersburg, later called Petrograd (now Leningrad), overshadows the dull greyness of post-revolutionary buildings. It's stunning. Leningrad stacks up with Paris as one of the most beautiful cities in the world — Old Leningrad, I mean, not the monotonous, uninspiring rows of high-rise apartments that characterize the suburbs, where our huge, new hotel was located.

By the time a tourist has visited the Hermitage, one of

A visit to the Winter Palace and the Hermitage with Inna, one of our national guides.

It Takes More Than One City to Know Russia 17

People-watching on Nevsky Prospekt.

the finest art museums in the world, and marveled at its lavishly furnished rooms, he is totally captivated. And that's just for starters.

The Hermitage collection is so large it is housed in two buildings, the Winter Palace, restored after the great fire of 1839, and the new Hermitage constructed from 1839 to 1852 near the palace. The museum's display of some 65,000 works of art occupies some 400 rooms, including "the largest assemblage of French Impressionists anywhere in the world." Italian masterpieces include Raphael's *Constabile Madonna,* Titian's *Magdalene Repentant,* and in a room housing the works of famed Dutch and Flemish artists I counted at least 25 paintings by Rembrandt, including *The Return of the Prodigal Son.*

Being people-oriented, Shirley and I got our biggest thrill standing on a corner of Leningrad's main street, Nevsky Prospekt, and watching the people. We've often described our first experiences in the Soviet Union as a dream come true, and watching the throngs of people rushing past us — ignoring our movie camera as if it were an everyday sight instead of a rarity — enhanced the dream.

To the folks at Intourist, we must have seemed like a couple of oddballs. Imagine anyone preferring to stand on a street corner instead of lingering with the symbols of Russia's heritage — magnificent old churches and cathedrals no longer in use except as museums. Never in a million years would anyone have answered the obvious question we might have asked but didn't: How many ex-houses-of-worship could a person visit in this atheistic state?

Although adults ignored us without exception, several young people armed with radios or stereo players that blared out rock and roll music stopped us ostensibly to chat. Some spoke English fluently, some haltingly. Their real object wasn't idle conversation. Either they wanted to trade rubles for American dollars on the black market

It Takes More Than One City to Know Russia 19

exchange or buy any item of clothing we would sell them, so they could turn around and sell those items for a profit.

Having been forewarned, we would tell them we had nothing to buy or sell and they would disappear. No high pressure tactics, no unpleasantness to mar those first impressions.

If we had left this magnificent city and flown back to New York three or four days later, we would have had fond remembrances of Leningrad that soon would have dimmed. But we never would have known Russia, any more than a foreign visitor would know America just by visiting New York City.

CHAPTER 5

A PROFESSOR HELPS SOLVE A MYSTERY

WHEN WE VISITED Peter the Great's magnificent summer palace outside Leningrad, we were overwhelmed in two ways. The beauty of the palace itself and the countless acres of manicured grounds and imposing fountains almost left us speechless. Although taking photographs inside wasn't permitted, my TV camera recorded the outside scenery for posterity. Peter the Great, who was responsible for most of Leningrad's beautiful architecture, outdid himself with his summer palace.

So much for history. Within moments after our tour was over, we were overwhelmed in a totally different way. Inna, one of our national Intourist guides, led us toward the restrooms. She stopped within some 50 feet of them and said, "Be prepared for culture shock." The remark went over our heads at first. The experience made believers of us. Never in our travels, including the most remote parts of China, India, New Guinea, and stretches of the camel-trodden Sinai Desert, had we been hit by such an odor.

A Professor Helps Solve a Mystery 21

What genius creates, clods foul up, we decided, thinking this abomination was caused by the apparent theft of all the plumbing valves by inconsiderate parties unknown. We were wrong. The smell in the public toilet facilities at the plush Leningrad opera that evening was every bit as offensive. The same went for the restrooms on the main floor of our 20-story Intourist hotel in Moscow.

Plush but no flush. I resolved to get to the bottom of this mystery if I had to insult every public official I met. I knew I couldn't pin the blame on Russian practical jokers. The ordinary Russian can go to the museums and the opera houses, but he can't get inside an Intourist hotel unless he's on official government business. Even Intourist guests can't enter their hotels without a hotel identification, which is given out at the registration desk.

With one quick deduction, I exonerated 260 million suspects out of the Soviet Union's 280 million population. The other 20 million, most of whom are members of the elitist Communist Party, were still under suspicion.

I brought up the subject with bureaucrats, professors and journalists, first in Moscow, then in Kiev and Odessa. In Odessa, my crusade was given new life after we went to the opera. Odessa's opera house ranks as one of the five most beautiful in the world, including our Met and La Scala. But the smell in the toilets is ranker than any.

None of the people I queried wanted to talk about it. They gave me a jaundiced eye, which I didn't know what to do with because I already had two jaundiced eyes busily following my nose for news.

Thanks to the accidental help of Dr. Alexander Volchenko, a professor of medicine at the Crimean Medical Institute in Simferopol, I solved the mystery to my own satisfaction. *The culprit is the class system in the world's most stratified society.* Dr. Volchenko, who sat between Shirley and me at dinner in Yalta, confessed that he never visited Russia's public toilet facilities. He lived in his own world of private offices, private restaurants, private floors in hotels, and private restrooms kept spotless and odorless by custodians.

Dr. Volchenko said that this was the first time anyone to his knowledge had ever brought up the subject of the odorous public facilities. "You know how immaculate our streets are kept." Then he added thoughtfully, "Maybe we ought to bring some of those workers off the streets and use them to clean up the toilets."

"You got it, Doc," I responded. I started to tell him about the babushka in Communist Bulgaria who stood guard over a men's public restroom and raked in a small fortune by charging admission. Just so she wouldn't appear too capitalistic in that Iron Curtain communist country, she refused to take American money.

Instead, I commented that in our travels in the Soviet Union, I had seen only one washroom attendant. "That was in Moscow. He wasn't there to clean or flush. He just sat and handed out paper towels."

I knew that Dr. Volchenko was an important man. He had appeared on the panel at our Yalta Hotel along with an English professor and the Communist spokesman, Dr. Ivanian. But Dr. Volchenko had assured us that he was not a member of the Communist Party. I don't know whether or not he was able to do anything about getting babushkas and elderly men off the streets and into the toilets with their brooms and mops, or whether he forgot about the "problem" 10 minutes after we parted.

I don't think I'll call and ask him.

CHAPTER 6

FIRST NEWS STORY GAVE US A BAD MOMENT

OUR COPIES of *Newsweek, Time, The Wall Street Journal* and other current news material from America were confiscated by the Leningrad airport customs inspectors on our arrival in the Soviet Union from Helsinki.

We didn't know it then, but for the next full month we were to face a Paper Curtain as well as the infamous Iron Curtain we'd heard so much about. Except for two English language propaganda tabloids, one published daily in London by the Communist Party affiliate, *The Daily Worker*, and the other published twice weekly in Moscow by the government-run Novosti Agency, we lived with a news blackout.

It was probably just as well. Our first encounter with Soviet-style journalism nearly gave us a group heart attack. On the bus, one of our traveling companions circulated a copy of the London tabloid. He'd circled the front page lead story with his pen.

To our dismay, we learned that "due to the falling dollar, America was facing total financial disaster following an economic crash of huge proportions." Illustrated by a vintage 1932 file photo of Americans standing in breadlines, the story spelled out the gory details of "the worst economic recession to hit the United States since the Great Depression."

"My God, this is dated today, Tuesday," someone said. "I wish I could get to a telephone and call home."

Just before the panic set in, an observant publisher who had probably started as a proofreader, shouted, "Hey, wait a minute. This paper is dated Tuesday all right. But not today. It's two weeks old. If I remember correctly, we were all back in the United States preparing for this trip. Does anyone remember anything about a stock market crash and all these gory details?"

"No!" we responded in unison.

A voice from the back of the bus said: "I bought this paper at the hotel this morning before we left. I wonder if I can get my kopecks back."

That early experience was a good lesson to us. Not only did we observe the datelines on the tabloids we continued to buy at hotel newsstands and kiosks all across the Soviet Union, but we also ignored the headlines. The old axiom that there's nothing as old as yesterday's newspaper didn't apply to Russia. The sheer logistics of getting anything on time in the world's largest nation might be excuse enough for selling papers that were at least two or three weeks older than yesterday. As if logistics really served as an excuse for inefficiency. . . .

What was inexcusable though was the anti-American propaganda that the Soviet Union's only available English language newspapers foisted on their readers.

A typical news story in the Soviet press would go something like this: "Yesterday, the American government committed a dastardly deed for which it will never be forgiven. . . ."

According to the ethics we were taught in journalism school, that's a no-no for the news columns. Such comments are reserved for columnists and editorial writers.

Without lofty principles, which American journalism for the most part lives up to better than all the rest of the world, we wouldn't have lofty comments such as this anonymous one in a letter to Colonel Edward Carrington (Jan. 16, 1787):

"... were it left to me to decide whether we should have a government without newspapers, or newspapers without a government, I should not hesitate a moment to prefer the latter."

What a laugh such a statement would give the boys in the Kremlin!

CHAPTER 7

RUSSIAN "PRIZES" BEAT THE PULITZER

DESPITE ITS many faults, the American press tries to present the news objectively. One of the first things pounded into the heads of students in our journalism schools is the difference between news and editorial commentaries or personal columns.

We weren't naive enough to be shocked at the way the role of journalism was viewed by Russian educators when we visited Leningrad University. Objectivity is scarcely considered. What counts is telling it like the government wants it to be told, not like it is.

Our host, Deputy Director Ivanovitch, presided over a panel of department heads, including the chairman of the journalism school, a former bureau chief for *Pravda*. Unlike the hard sciences such as mathematics and physics, whose integrity is respected, journalism and history are viewed as tools of the communist system.

Yet, good old Leningrad U. journalists are looked upon

as key figures in the success or failure of the Soviet system. Said Mr. Ivanovitch blithely, "Candidates for our journalism school are selected and graded on the basis of their devotion to Lenin's principles. Those who do the best job of motivating the nation's workers and collective farmers to promote socialism better, are the gifted ones who are invited to join the Communist Party."

What does belonging to that elite minority of less than 20 million persons out of the Soviet Union's 280 million population mean to a Russian journalist? Officially, of course, one of Lenin's basic tenets was the classless society. Unofficially, party members and other V.I.P.'s, including stars of sports, the ballet and opera, distinguished writers, scientists, and airline pilots, lead the life of Riley, not Lenin. The Father of the Russian Revolution would be turning in his glass-covered tomb if he knew that the classless society now grants these and other fringe benefits to the privileged:

1. Chauffeur-driven limousines.
2. A summer home.
3. Special housing.
4. Special places to eat, shop and play.
5. Special privileges to travel abroad.
6. And, most importantly, a special permit to enter the private washrooms throughout Russia that remain off-limits to the underprivileged masses.

Leningrad University, one of the nation's oldest, dating back to the early 1800s, graduates about 100 journalists a year. Three out of every five who complete the five-year course go to work for newspapers or periodicals. The others serve at television or radio stations. Needless to say, none of them pound the streets selling advertising because everything belongs to the government. With no competition, who needs to fight for customers?

Mr. Ivanovitch and the head of the journalism school who used to work for *Pravda* ("Truth"), acted as if they just couldn't understand why we American newspaper publishers turned thumbs down on the Soviet educational program for would-be journalists.

To their credit, they didn't say it, but we knew they wondered what a handful of capitalistic publishers could possibly know about selfless dedication to such a noble cause as promoting Lenin's ideals.

While we were still pursuing foolish goals like Pulitzer prizes, they were taking a more pragmatic approach to rewarding the gifted. And, after all, how could a few fringe benefits corrupt the integrity and loyalty of a dyed-in-the-wool Leningrad University trained propagandist? I'm sure they pitied us for being so naive.

CHAPTER 8

THE UNIONS TAKE OVER AS PROXY PARENTS

SOONER OR LATER, everything must get down to the children. They are the future of every nation. But in the Soviet Union, powerful forces outside the family are shaping the future by first molding the minds of little children.

That the youngsters are treated well seems obvious. They are dressed nicely, have plenty to eat, get good educations — and more than their fill of regimentation. And they accept the regimentation without public protest, if they protest at all. In the strict Soviet society, there is no room for individual thought, individual initiative, or above all, individual temperament.

Many times, we observed children in groups — at museums, circuses, or walking together with their teachers. Their silent, unemotional obedience reminded us more of mechanical dolls than real, live boys and girls. Nobody held up the procession, nobody straggled behind, nobody complained or whimpered, nobody daydreamed like little kids do elsewhere in the world.

Painting of Lenin at the entrance of pre-school.

The Unions Take Over as Proxy Parents   31

At the fabulous Moscow Children's Theatre where they are taught by professional entertainers to understand and appreciate opera, ballet and symphonic music, the children behaved like model adults. They were quiet, attentive, obedient. Inside an auditorium, we watched as they responded on cue to questions from the stage and applauded with the strange, staccato rhythm so unique to Soviet audiences. Only rarely did we hear a spontaneous laugh from any of them.

We were taken to a large day care center and pre-school in Odessa — modern and spotlessly clean, with facilities for children from infancy through age seven when they start regular school. The center is financed and operated by a trade union in a nearby factory. All the youngsters are children of workers at that factory. All will grow up to be workers at that factory someday. The government-controlled union has decided that. Only an especially gifted child may hope to rise above his stratified level and be chosen for a higher position in life. . . .

We took seats in an all-purpose room and watched with pleasure as some two dozen boys and girls between the ages of five and seven presented a program especially for our group. As Lenin peered down from the wall, the children, dressed in colorful costumes of the Ukraine (the breadbasket of Russia where Odessa is located), marched, sang and danced to the Ukrainian music played by a woman pianist. Another woman studiously supervised the presentation.

But the children needed no supervision. They didn't miss a beat. Their minds didn't wander. The only thing unusual to us was their lack of expression. Only one youngster, a strikingly pretty girl, smiled. When the program was over, the young people dutifully came over to our group. Each picked out a partner, the pianist started to play, and everyone danced the chicken dance to a tune known all over the world.

How similar the reactions were among us as we com-

School children on an outing.

The Unions Take Over as Proxy Parents

We were greeted at the Odessa pre-school by children in the traditional dress of the Ukraine.

Pupils performing for our group.

The Unions Take Over as Proxy Parents

pared notes later.

"If a fly had landed on each child's nose, not a single hand would have brushed it off."

"Those guards at Lenin's tomb would probably give out medals to those kids."

A woman complained, "I danced with a handsome little boy and tried my darndest to get him to look at me. He wouldn't take his eyes off the floor, and his face never showed the slightest emotion. He wasn't scared stiff. I was."

Maybe in their homes, away from the structured, almost paramilitary environment of this innocent-looking children's center, those youngsters cut loose. Maybe they laugh and giggle and do crazy things and even get into trouble sometimes just like children in every other country do.

But in the brief period those kids are away from the center, there may not be time for them to come to life with their real parents. Maybe what they are and will become will be shaped by their proxy parents — the trade union.

CHAPTER 9

GOOSE-STEPPING SOLDIERS— A POWERFUL REMINDER

IT'S NOT SUCH a great distinction, but I just might be the only American who ever sat behind Lenin's desk. I don't know what possessed me to plop down in his chair. Let's just say a guy from Ohio egged me on . . . the devil made him do it.

The picture taken with our camera by our fellow publisher, is priceless to me. It isn't often that Shirley is caught with her hand in the cookie jar.

If there is such a thing as a sacrilegious act in the atheistic Soviet Union, then I must plead guilty. But Angelina Kontchorova, who recovered from shock long enough to pose for a picture with Shirley, must have forgiven me. And that's what counts. After all, the pretty lady is historian of the Smolny Institute in Leningrad, a museum that exhibits Vladimir Lenin's tiny office and the rest of his apartment, where I committed the alleged crime.

Smolny used to be an exclusive girls' school before Lenin and his pals seized it and made it revolutionary

Goose-Stepping Soldiers—A Powerful Reminder

"Caught in the act..."

—PHOTO BY MAYNARD BUCK

headquarters.

Ah Lenin! When other names are long forgot, his will still be hot. Stalin and Khrushchev have been erased from memory by official edict. Marx and Engels have faded into history through journalistic neglect. But Lenin, the father of the Russian Revolution, waxes stronger with each day, and no pun is intended.

Embalmed in a glass covered casket in a large marble tomb, his body lies in state in Moscow's Red Square. Millions of Russians and foreign tourists annually make the pilgrimage to his shrine, some out of devotion but most out of respect or curiosity. Sometimes the wait lasts for hours. The tomb is open daily only from 10 A.M. to about 2 P.M., so it was not a surprise to us to learn that the line forms 10 blocks away.

None of us doubted that since his death in 1924, Vladimir Lenin, born Vladimir Ilyich Ulyanov, has been "officially" installed as the God of Godless Russia.

Although soldiers are on duty everywhere in gigantic Red Square, the tomb itself is guarded only by two soldiers standing at rigid attention in front of the doors. These young men are the cream of Russia's military crop, chosen for their endurance and self-discipline. They do not move.

The changing of the guard takes place every hour on the hour as the clock in the Kremlin tower bongs deeply, in keeping with the solemn occasion. As we watched at 11 o'clock at night, the scene was awesome. Lights played on the red flag high above the tower as it waved in the breeze, a hush fell over the entire square, and from a gate at the Kremlin wall came the new guard, accompanied by escorts. They didn't march to the tomb, they *goose-stepped*. When the watch was relieved from duty, the retiring guard was escorted back to the Kremlin gate, every soldier goose-stepping all the way.

Funny that Russians should be goose-stepping. Visions of marching Nazi soldiers popped into our heads. Not a

Goose-Stepping Soldiers—A Powerful Reminder

. . . but all is forgiven.

Lenin's sitting room.

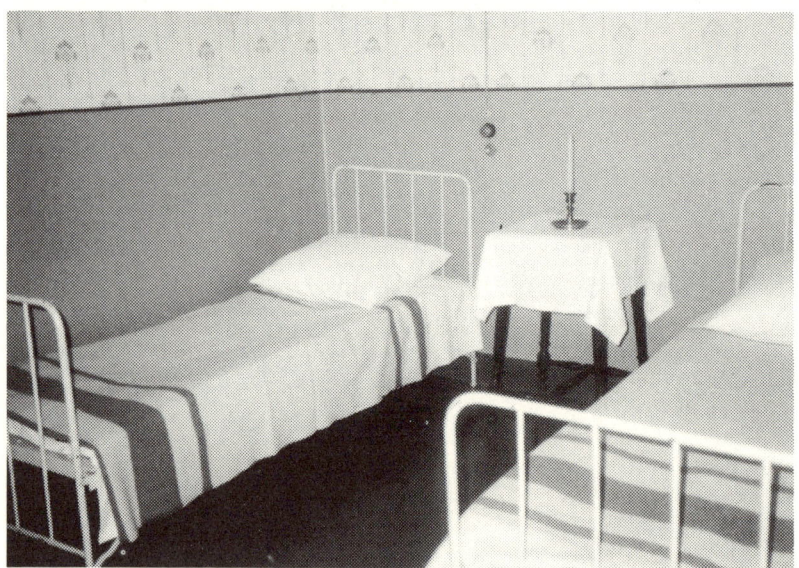
His bedroom.

Goose-Stepping Soldiers—A Powerful Reminder

Crowds waiting to visit Lenin's tomb.

day passes that the Russian people are not reminded of the Nazi invaders, the slaughter of 20 million Russians by Nazi soldiers. To us, World War II happened 40 years ago. To the Russians it happened yesterday. Why, we asked ourselves, as we traveled across the country, seeing Soviet soldiers marching even in parades like carbon copies of the Nazis, did the people need this sordid reminder of one of the saddest chapters in their history?

Did goose-stepping make these youngsters in uniform more fearsome? Did it give the Russian army an aura of power? Did it add to the message the Kremlin wants all the world to know and never lets it forget: "Russian military might will protect its people from the nuclear attack that will surely be launched by the United States."

I guess a world that sees the daily soap opera unfold in Russia will swallow what the Kremlin wants it to believe. I guess the majority of Russians are swallowing it too. Yet, there were times when we'd get more than a hint as we traveled through the Soviet Union that a lot of people weren't as gullible as they appeared to be. There were times we were almost sure many knew that the Kremlin alarms were hogwash, that those goose-stepping kids in uniform didn't like playing soldier.

And that Lenin isn't God, he's just Peasant under Glass.

But they play the game because they are boxed in. And they console themselves and their children that even at its worst, life under communism is more bearable than it was under the czars, under the Turks, under the Mongols, and under the Nazi boot.

Goose-Stepping Soldiers—A Powerful Reminder

Goose-stepping soldiers eye our camera.

Splendor of Lenin's headquarters belied his simple taste.

CHAPTER 10

PECTOPAH—THE McDONALD'S OF RUSSIA?

"**W**HO IS THIS GUY Pectopah?" I asked one morning on the bus. "He must own more restaurants than McDonald's."

The comment drew a laugh, which goes to prove how little rest we were getting. A woman in our group went so far as to explain that pectopah is the Russian word for restaurant. "The letter *p* in Russian is *r* in English: *e* is *e*, *c* is *s*, *t* is *t*, *o* is *o*, *a* is *a*, and *h* is pronounced *a-n*," our patient traveling companion continued.

"Put them all together and they spell *restarah'n*."

Our tutor was too late. From that moment on, pectopah became pectopah wherever we went. Russia needs more inside jokes. Russia needs more jokes, period. Among other things, there's a shortage of laughter except at the circus.

There were pectopah signs all over Moscow and Leningrad. One of the best we visited was within walking distance of the Kremlin. Coincidentally, Moscow was one of the few places where our tight schedule allowed us time to go out to dinner.

This particular pectopah was crammed with Russian diners, and we didn't see a single tourist. Our friends from Ohio (names withheld to protect the innocent who are not responsible for the views expressed in this book) had prepaid at our Intourist hotel for our dinners and were hosting us.

They had picked out a pre-set menu that started with caviar and cabbage borscht, continued with an entree of roast beef and browned potatoes, and ice cream for dessert. A bottle of Stolichnaya vodka and a bottle of champagne were awaiting our arrival. And, of course, a heaping plate of Russia's delicious black bread was refilled two or three times.

We sat down to eat a well-prepared meal. It would be duplicated in some hotel dining rooms all through Russia, but because of the atmosphere, the music, and the fact that we were surrounded by real Russians, this meal was special.

The other diners weren't bureaucrats. Just plain, ordinary Russians. A bureaucrat wouldn't be found dead in a pectopah like this.

About 50 or 60 Russians were celebrating a family wedding, and as they began to sing and dance, we got up from our table, glasses in hand, and walked across the room to toast them. The handsome young bride and groom couldn't have been more than teenagers. We learned from the manager that the wedding ceremony had been performed at the Marriage Palace just that afternoon.

Russians aren't married in the church. They are united in holy (?) matrimony at a plush, government-operated Marriage Palace, which some in our group said resembles the wedding chapels in Las Vegas and Reno. A civil ceremony is conducted by a duly authorized official, beneath the framed photograph or painting of a beaming Vladimir Lenin.

The shy young groom at the pectopah didn't hesitate to

Pectopah—The McDonald's of Russia? 49

oblige those who began to chant "gorko, gorko" ("kiss the bride"). As he kissed his willing mate, we joined in a toast. Many at the party smiled at us and made us feel welcome. Soon we were clapping our hands in rhythmic cadence as is so commonplace at gatherings throughout the Soviet Union. For that evening, we weren't party crashers. We felt right at home. What we didn't know then but learned later is that Russians seldom let down their guard during the daytime. If we'd have run across any in that crowd the next day, they would have acted as if they had never seen us before.

But for those few hours, we felt we had broken a barrier. As we prepared to leave, our companion from Ohio offered our half-filled bottle of vodka to a couple at the next table. They smiled and accepted the gift graciously.

The next night in Moscow, Intourist entertained us at a stuffy and more elaborate pectopah that was jammed with tourists. After we left the capital, most of our meals for the next few weeks were served at hotels.

Pectopahs in the rest of the Soviet Union were few and far between, darn it.

CHAPTER 11

CHET GIVES US A HOT SCOOP ON AFGHANISTAN

NONE OF OUR GROUP of journalists was medically qualified to call two Soviet diplomats paranoid, but most came to that conclusion independently after meeting with them.

The scene was the Soviet Ministry of Foreign Affairs in Moscow on an early October morning. Pessimism quickly filled the air as the chief spokesman, the minister in charge of United States Affairs, predicted that little or nothing would be accomplished at the November summit in Geneva.

Then he went on to blame the United States for almost everything going wrong in the world. In flawless English, Sergei Chetverikov — "They called me Chet during the years I was assigned to the Soviet Embassy in Washington" — continued his verbal attack.

"America's purpose in meddling in other countries is to push us around and try to squeeze us out of the world economy. We won't be pushed around," Chet said.

"You ask why we are in Afghanistan? We are there

Chet Gives Us a Hot Scoop on Afghanistan

because your country was planning to build a giant air base that would enable it to dominate Afghanistan and endanger our security. We were asked by the government of Afghanistan to send our troops and save them from American imperialism. We had no other choice....

"American leaders don't want us to get out of Afghanistan. President Reagan wants this to be our Vietnam....

"When your country interferes in other countries, invades Grenada and dictates to El Salvador and Nicaragua, it is fostering wars to make profits for the arms makers. When the Soviets assist in the liberation of other nations, we do it for noble reasons."

As we would later learn, the Soviets spread that poison from Moscow, to all parts of the Soviet Union daily through its government-controlled press, government-controlled radio, government-controlled schools. It may be old stuff to Americans, but the Communist Party takes no chances on anyone in the USSR forgetting who the enemy is supposed to be.

What I'm about to tell you, however, is not old stuff. At least, it was not when we first heard it October 1, at the Soviet Ministry of Foreign Affairs. As we had learned to do in press visits to the Middle East, the Iron Curtain countries and other hot spots, Shirley and I lagged behind after the conference to chat briefly with the two Soviet diplomats. Two or three members of our group went with us.

We exchanged calling cards first with the other panelist, Vladimir A. Morozov, deputy chief of the Soviet Press Department, whom we had difficulty in understanding because of his halting English. Then we traded cards with "Chet." His grumpiness, which no doubt was the official posture he regularly took when speaking to foreign groups, disappeared. He glanced at my small TV camera which I'd used to record the panel discussion and suddenly responded to a comment I had dared to make to him. "Mr. Minister, most readers of this group's newspapers in

Private chat with Mr. Morozov and Chet.

Chet Gives Us a Hot Scoop on Afghanistan

America want peace. They believe you have other than noble reasons for being in Afghanistan. Do you agree you may have lost your credibility with them and other people in the world over this war in Afghanistan?"

Chetverikov's response shocked all of us within hearing range. "There is no doubt about it. We have got to get out of Afghanistan. It is draining our youth and undermining our credibility as a peace-loving nation. The problem is we don't know how to get out."

At the American Embassy in Moscow that same afternoon, I reported what Chet had told us to a State Department official who had just briefed us on the latest development in the Soviet Union. The official, who asked not to be identified, couldn't conceal his surprise at Chetverikov's statement.

Not once until the conclusion of the summit talks in Geneva on November 21 did we see or hear public mention in the media or elsewhere that would indicate a change of position on Afghanistan by the Soviet Union. But I believe the message we relayed to that official at the United States Embassy in Moscow went right to the State Department in Washington and on to the White House.

If so, the foreknowledge may have provided President Reagan with an opening to suggest that Secretary General Gorbachev withdraw his troops from Afghanistan. He has since turned that suggestion into an official request.

Don't be surprised if one of the first major developments to follow the historic Geneva Summit will be the announcement one day that the Soviet Union has found a way to pull out of the quicksand of you know where. . . .

CHAPTER 12

INFLEXIBLE RULES WIN OUT IN THE END

WELL-MEANING FOLKS can sure cause headaches sometimes.

The helpful lady at the bank in our hometown suggested that I sign each of the American Express travelers checks on the top line and add the name of my home town beside the signature. I complied.

Little did I know what a mess I'd be in when I tried to cash those checks in Russia — anywhere in Russia.

The nyets we'd heard at the service bureaus and other stops were nothing compared to the nyets we got at the cashier windows in hotels and banks when we presented one of those checks.

With the nyets would come a stream of Russian words which I didn't understand but was sure amounted to a declaration of war. How was I going to persuade these rigid women who knew enough English to tell me they would not cash the checks, that they ought to be sweet and change their minds? After all, I was a nice American tourist who wasn't going to run off with stolen Soviet

Inflexible Rules Win Out in the End 55

rubles that weren't worth anything out of the country. Besides, my passport, as always, was in the possession of the registration desk.

Pleading didn't get the job done and neither did sweet talk. I sent for our guides on several occasions and asked their help. They had about as much clout with the cashiers as a Russian dissident seeking a visa to move to New York. Once, I asked for the hotel manager's help and an officious young man showed up. The cashier nearly chewed him up. She didn't take orders from him, she took orders from headquarters. Headquarters said you signed only your name at the top, not somebody else's name.

The manager, with our guide and interpreter Nadia's assistance, hastened to assure the cashier that Prairie Village, Kansas, wasn't the name of a person. The news didn't budge her.

Realizing they had no authority over these minor bureaucrats who were accountable to nobody except their superiors in Moscow, the hotel managers and Intourist guides would desert me in my hour of need.

I managed to get three or four $25 or $50 checks cashed by standing in front of the window and refusing to budge. I wore down the resistance of a few cashiers, who, after all, were just doing their duty by inflexible Moscow standards. Beyond that, I managed to get by with my limited cash. In Japan, those worthless checks suddenly became legal tender again with no questions asked.

Shirley wasn't as fortunate in fighting the country's inflexible rules, and nearly wound up with pneumonia. At the opera in Leningrad one chilly evening shortly after our arrival in the Soviet Union, she wanted to keep her coat on because she was coming down with a cold. For some reason, which nobody ever explained to us, Russian rules require that everyone attending a public event indoors must check his coat. That goes for operas, ballets, circuses, and other forms of entertainment. There is no charge for checking and everyone meekly complies with the rules.

But Shirley said "Nyet" to the checking, even though normally she would not have questioned the rules. The hitch came when she tried to take her seat. A stern attendant refused to let her enter our box until her coat was checked. She waited outside while I ran downstairs and checked the coat. The opera house was cold. Shirley began to sneeze. Fortunately, her cold lasted only a couple of days, leaving her posing the question, "In Muslim lands, we had to take off our shoes before entering a mosque. In Japan, we took off our shoes before entering a pagoda or a home. It is understandable to respect religious customs. But Russia is a country that respects no religion. Why should we take off our coats?"

CHAPTER 13

STORES EXCEL IN ORGANIZED INEFFICIENCY

By Shirley Rose

ANY RESEMBLANCE between Mrs. Gorbachev's outfits and the clothes we saw in the shops in the Soviet Union is strictly coincidental. Just out of curiosity we went up and down Gorky Street, the main street in Moscow, to see the stores' fashions and how prices compared with ours.

The dresses in the windows and on the racks were so inferior in quality as well as design that our women would consign them to the thrift shops. The prices were ridiculous.

In every country we had visited on five continents, we found that prices in the tourist shops were considerably higher than in the department stores. In Russia the opposite is true.

One could buy a fur hat, fox or mink, in a Beriozka (tourist store) for about $100. The same hats in the department stores were priced at about 400 rubles. Four hundred rubles on the Russian exchange is equal to about

Shoe repair shop holds one customer at a time.

Stores Excel in Organized Inefficiency

500 American dollars. You see, Russians can't shop at tourist shops. They all have to shop at the "company" store because that is the only place where rubles are worth anything. They are government stores and the prices are set by the government. No competition, no sales, and no service.

Customer "service" was the most organized inefficiency I have ever seen.

I tried to buy a can of hair spray in Odessa at the local department store. I went to the counter and pointed to a can of spray. The lady behind the counter handed me the can. Since I had seen what I thought was a check-out stand, I proceeded to get in the line to pay for the hair spray. Suddenly, the saleslady came up behind me and grabbed the can of hair spray out of my hand with no attempt to explain by word or gesture.

I was stunned, but realized I must be doing something wrong so I went back to the counter. This time the lady frowned and showed me the price of the can and pointed to one of the waiting lines. I didn't know the amount I should pay but decided to chance it with a few gestures. I got into a line when all of the sudden the same saleslady started shouting at me. No one tried to help as had been done in China, for example. I decided it wasn't worth it and left the store without the spray.

Later, at the hotel service bureau, someone explained that when you want to make a purchase of any kind you must let the saleslady know what you want, get the price of the item, stand in the proper line to pay for it, get a sales slip showing you have paid, go back to another line where the saleslady then will give you the item after accepting your sales slip.

What would take me five or ten minutes to purchase in one of our stores takes at least fifteen or twenty minutes if the lines are not too long. Repeat this process when you grocery shop. And add to it the inconvenience of going to a different shop for different items and you can see how frustrating it must be for the Russian housewife to do her shopping. There is a dairy store, a meat store, a fish store, a bakery shop, etc., etc.

In far-off Khabarovsk, just across the river from China, we wanted to get something to serve to our group at a farewell get-together in our tiny room. We went by a bakery at about two o'clock, but it had not yet opened for the day. We noticed that a truck was unloading baked goods so we decided that we would try again later. About four o'clock the door was opened and a crowd of people poured into the little shop.

The baked goods were in bins. There were no salesladies and no counters, so I took six giant-sized bagels in my hands. There were no bags or paper in which to wrap the bagels.

At the check-out counter, the cashier, using the usual abacus, looked up, told me the amount of my purchase, took my money and dismissed me.

We walked about six or seven blocks to the hotel with those bagels in my hands, my pockets, in Stan's hands and his pockets. On the way, we bought flowers from a stand in the cold of Siberia to enhance the festive occasion that would highlight one last evening in the Soviet Union.

CHAPTER 14

RULES OR NOT, TIPPING IS A WAY OF LIFE

TIPPING IS officially prohibited in the USSR. But there's always some son of a gun who doesn't get the word. Gorbachev may flip when he hears this, but his country is full of such sons of guns, and I say that affectionately.

It wasn't until I was told by a wise "fellow traveler" to tip the key lady that we finally got a call through from Russia to Kansas City. There were times, at first, when we would try to put a call through ourselves, but we would always be frustrated by a number of obstacles: (1) We couldn't reach the long-distance operator, (2) We couldn't reach any operator, (3) When we would reach an operator, one of the following would happen: (a) She couldn't hear us, (b) We couldn't hear her, (c) She could hear but would tell us to call back tomorrow because either the lines were busy or she was busy, (d) She would promise to make the connection and notify us as soon as our party was reached. We would obediently hang up and never hear from her again.

Like Russian telephone operators, Russian key ladies speak English, of sorts. But money talks in any language. Having been unable to call anyone from Leningrad and Moscow, in Kiev — or was it Odessa? — I approached the key lady on our hotel floor, put a couple of rubles in her hand and gave her the telephone number.

The middle-aged woman beamed, dutifully protesting that it wasn't necessary to give her money, put the rubles in her pocket and reached for the phone. "I will let you know exactly what time your call will be ready in case there is a delay," she said. I went back to the room.

The phone rang minutes later. Our call to the United States was ready. It was nine hours earlier back home and we had awakened some sleeping people, but they were happy and relieved to hear our voices. Everyone was fine, and newswise, the Kansas City Royals were still tied for first place with California in the Western Division in the American League pennant race. We wouldn't learn for several weeks — when we arrived in Japan — that Kansas City would go on to win the 1985 World Series.

Afterward I went to thank the key lady and offered her another couple of rubles for performing her miracle. She refused them. "You have given me enough already," she said. I tried to remember when I'd heard anything like that before. Never. I wanted to hug the woman, but I was afraid she might break my arm. So I shook her hand instead.

After that, I became a regular tipper. I tipped almost everywhere except in the special dining rooms where only our small group was served.

My tips were always accepted without surprise. Even though we visited some remote places in the Soviet Union, some tourist with a tip had always been there before us. Once, I reached in my pocket to reward an elderly porter but didn't have any Russian money. I handed the man an American dollar bill. I thought the fellow would faint. He not only thanked us warmly ("spasibo! spasibo!"), but actually backed out of the room bowing.

Rules or Not, Tipping Is a Way of Life

With those foreign dollars and the right connections, the Russian people manage to buy things at the special tourist stores, even items seldom available in their own stores. If they were available, they would cost several times as much in rubles as in dollars. They are not permitted to enter the Beriozka where only foreign money is accepted, but they have connections if they have the right money.

Forbidding such capitalistic practices as tipping may be good points from a moralistic standpoint, but the Soviet leadership has to face up to the facts of life. Their society is becoming more and more dependent on tourism, but it goes out of its way to promote poor service. In defense, foreign tourists are resorting more and more to following the international custom of tipping to ensure some kind of service.

Furthermore, a society that rips off its own people more flagrantly than it rips off its tourists should know that it has ensured that tipping will become a way of life between Russian and Russian, as well as between foreign tourist and Russian. The alternative is that nobody will get any service, and that's just what is happening!

CHAPTER 15

THE ICEBREAKER STRIKES AGAIN
By Shirley Rose

SIX YEARS AGO when we went to China, I took along my Polaroid camera because we felt it would be a fun thing to do and a way for us to communicate. It proved to be such an effective icebreaker that whenever we go any place where language is a barrier, we take along that Polaroid.

I didn't use it in Moscow, Leningrad or any of the more sophisticated cities. I'm sorry now that I didn't. But as soon as we arrived in the Ukraine, I took it out of the camera case. We would walk along the street by ourselves, smiling and trying to catch the eye of someone. But no luck. People would turn their backs and walk away.

At a market in Tashkent, a Soviet Republic near Afghanistan, I finally persuaded a girl to pose for me. She didn't understand one word I said, but with gestures I was able to make her understand the picture was for her. As the photograph developed, so did the crowd around us. From that moment until we left the market, we had a large entourage following us around.

Some ran to bring me flowers to show their appreciation for the pictures I gave them. It was a thrill to get through to them at last.

One Sunday in Irkutsk, Siberia, we joined people strolling along the promenade overlooking the river. I saw two babushkas and walked toward them. They turned their backs, but I persisted, and finally they allowed me to take a picture. I handed the finished photograph to one of the women. She was thrilled. The other lady started looking in her pocketbook. She tried to hand me a ruble so I would take another picture for her. I hastened to assure her she didn't need the ruble and took another picture for her. As she saw it develop, she suddenly gave me a big hug and kissed my cheek. Such unexpected warmth in her eyes made my heart pound with joy.

At Lake Baikal, near Irkutsk, we visited a little village where dirt roads and century-old houses offered quite a contrast to Siberian cities. We could hardly wait to take pictures. All of a sudden, everyone disappeared. The village was deserted. Finally, a woman came down the road toward us. She frowned at us and turned away.

A young man came out of a little general store, and I made him understand that we wanted to give him a picture. It was so cold that the usually quick developing process seemed to take forever. The man was very patient, and as the smile in the picture emerged so did the smile on his face.

I said, "All right?" He said, "All right." Nearby, a little girl and an elderly woman were curious to see what was going on. The man showed them the picture and explained to them what I was doing. They let me take their pictures, and, miraculously, the village suddenly came to life. People talked to us, people smiled, people shook

Polaroid candids made instant friends.

The Icebreaker Strikes Again

And, more friends!

hands. My camera clicked. In the cold, I kept saying, "It's coming, it's coming, the picture is going to be fine." They didn't understand the words, but they got the message and for the first time we were communicating. We couldn't sit down and say, "How do you like Russia?" because there was that real language barrier and they wouldn't have told us anyway. But at least we exchanged smiles.

I gave away about a hundred Polaroid pictures and never kept one. Such demand! I always made a point of saying "America" as I handed someone his picture. I would point to myself, then to them and say "Russia" and put out my hand. They would shake my hand, smile warmly, and repeat "America . . . Da."

CHAPTER 16

GORBACHEV GIVES THEM SOMETHING TO LOOK FORWARD TO — 2 P.M.

SOVIET LEADER MIKHAIL GORBACHEV had his mind on loftier matters than the Russian drinking problem when he got home from the Geneva summit. In the months since he took command of the Communist Party's Central Committee, Mr. Gorbachev's main accomplishment in dealing with his nation's massive problems so far has been condensing the public drinking hours.

His new restrictions, which include keeping the bars and liquor stores closed until 2 o'clock in the afternoon, have met with mixed reactions from a usually servile population. Some Soviet citizens have solved the dilemma by drinking more in the allotted time. But in faraway areas such as Siberia, even officials often look the other way when the Gorbachev rules are ignored. . . .

Our group arrived at our hotel in Novosibirsk, Siberia, after a long delayed flight from Tashkent, a Central Asian city only a few miles from the Afghanistan border. We were quickly ushered into a large, crowded dining room and seated at two long tables smack in the middle of the action. No isolated special dining room for us this time.

It took us a while to realize this was Saturday night in Novosibirsk and that we were virtually the only foreigners in the room. The residents of the Soviet Union's fifth largest city (population about 1.5 million) were whooping it up in the best hotel in town. The only other hotel, our guides said, was crummy.

An orchestra was playing American rock music, people were dancing and drinking. And drinking. The tables were set as we had seen elsewhere, including public restaurants in larger cities. In front of each diner was placed a bottle of "Stoley" (Stolichnaya), Russia's finest and smoothest vodka, as well as a bottle of cheap Russian champagne. And the heartiest of drinkers would often top those off with a bottle of cognac.

As our group joined in the fun, I saw a flying object, resembling a frisbee, sail through the air. A split second later it crashed against the wall and broke into pieces. We stole glances at the table next to us as a very intoxicated man was being rebuked by his woman companion and another couple at the table. He appeared too drunk to notice us.

A couple of employees came over to talk with him. The man, anxious to demonstrate that alcohol hadn't affected his coordination, picked up another plate and, with a twist of his wrist, sent it sailing in the exact direction of the other one. It, too, hit the wall. Flying pieces of china landed harmlessly on the dining room floor at least a dozen feet away from the nearest diner. The youngish drunk seemed pleased at his accuracy.

The next thing we knew, two bouncers removed the protesting drunk and his companions, and the table was cleared and reset. However, other customers were seated somewhere else. The table stayed empty.

About half an hour later, two Soviet policemen came to

usher out another drunk for creating a mild disturbance. But all in all, it was a fun-filled Saturday night in Siberia, and our hearts were broken when we discovered next morning that some joy-killing bureaucrat thousands of miles away in Moscow had received the news and promptly ordered our national tour guides to keep us away from the people at all meals.

If we are to believe Mr. Gorbachev's words about getting his bogged-down nation moving, about motivating his people, ending waste and inefficiency, and improving the nation's miserable production record, he must really attack the reasons for Russia's refuge in chronic alcoholism.

Having disposed of religion, the Communist Party which Gorbachev heads knows darned well that vodka is now the opiate of its people. Getting "bombed" seems to be the only way the people can endure the drab, slavish routine that has made a mockery of the promises Moscow has made to them for more than six decades.

Before he can achieve his stated goals, Mikhail Gorbachev has the monumental task of giving his people something to look forward to besides 2 P.M.

CHAPTER 17

A MIRACLE LENIN HAD NO PART OF

THIS SEEMS AN APPROPRIATE TIME to tell you about a miracle that happened in Moscow. Miracles do happen in the Soviet Union, although I'm sure if the spokesmen at the Kremlin knew about this one, they would credit it to the spirit of Vladimir Lenin.

No way. If any human living or dead is going to get credit, it will have to be Gary Dobrovolsky, chief cameraman for the American Broadcasting Company in Moscow. But I suspect that Gary would readily admit he couldn't have done it alone. There had to be some divine guidance that led him to a solution to our video camera's battery charger problem after he had given up hope.

Gary was our court of last resort. We had visited camera repair shops by taxi from one end of Moscow to the other, probably seeing more of the giant capital in a couple of days than most Muscovites see in a year. At every stop, after standing in long lines that formed in the lobbies of the buildings in which the repair shops were located, we would eventually inch our way up to the service windows.

There, white-uniformed women who looked more like surgeons than clerks would take our TV camera and battery charger, hand us a receipt and motion us to get out of line and wait. Language was superfluous.

As we found out at the very beginning of our expedition, the government-owned camera shops operate on a diagnosis-while-you-wait basis. Usually the verdict comes quickly. If the problem is minor, it is repaired on the spot for a nominal fee. If it is more serious but repairable, the customer is told when to return.

If that customer happens to be a Russian or one of countless other Soviet nationalities, before his camera is returned to him he must furnish proof of ownership and supply vital identification data contained in his domestic passport. Every Soviet must carry that passport with him at all times. It doesn't entitle him to travel abroad or even leave the community in which he lives, but it certainly makes it easier for the government to keep track of him.

Although we saw a few tourists on our Moscow adventure, most in line were Soviets. Despite the slowdown in service caused by the identification process, we enjoyed the waiting and watching. At decision time, we would always get the same answer: Nyet. The chief "surgeon" in a white uniform would shake his head, point to our TV camera, which he probably had never seen the likes of before, and to our burned-out battery charger, and repeat the last rites. Nyet, nyet, nyet.

Our battery charger was finished, dead, kaput. I hastily decided that October in the Soviet Union was going to be a lousy month for me. Once we left Moscow, where at least our batteries could be recharged until they burned out, I might as well kiss my precious TV camera goodbye. Without it, Siberia and the Trans-Siberian Railroad were going to be bummers.

Feeling sorry for myself, I had told my tale of woe to a high official at the American Embassy in Moscow. He was sympathetic but had no suggestions. Suddenly an idea

A Miracle Lenin had No Part Of

struck me. "Don't the American TV networks have bureaus here?"

The official got my message. He instructed his secretary to get me the addresses and phone numbers of the bureaus. The first one I called was ABC-TV, and I was put in touch immediately with the network's chief cameraman, Dobrovolsky, who listened and said he didn't know if he could help us but, "Come on over."

Gary, a bearded man in his mid-30s, fiddled with wires and fuses for about half an hour with no luck at all. The charger was beyond repair — in Russia, at least.

"Come on Gary, do something to make it work. Help a fellow American," I pleaded.

Gary winked. "I'm Canadian. I'll try one thing more."

In the fashion of that great American inventor, Rube Goldberg, Gary put together a contraption that included an old battery charger he found in a box and a couple of sets of positive and negative cables. Back at the hotel, we held our breaths as we tried to remember his instructions.

The ABC-TV battery charger, which we hope is now back in Gary's hands after it was mailed from our office early in November, supplied power to our burned-out charger, which made it work and kept our batteries properly charged and usable throughout the Soviet Union in the weeks that followed.

The Miracle on 34th Street was small potatoes compared to the Miracle on Prospekt 13.

CHAPTER 18

BLACK MARKET HACK GETS A RANSOM FOR A RIDE

ARMED WITH FRESHLY-CHARGED batteries for our video camera, Shirley and I decided to skip the group tour to Lenin's tomb at Red Square and go later. Instead, we set out to pay an unannounced visit to the apartment of the Evgeny Yakir family. Their address, along with a brief biography of these dissidents whom some members of the Kansas City community had "adopted," had been furnished us, but the telephone number had been left out. We decided not to trust anyone at the hotel to get it for us.

After carefully concealing the Yakirs' name, we showed the address to a clerk at the service bureau and asked her to write it in Russian. We walked out into the sunshine of a pleasant, unseasonably warm October afternoon, tingling with the excitement of adventure. The train trip from Leningrad to Moscow had been tiring, aggravating the jet lag we were still suffering, but that was all behind us.

A sea of taxis engulfed the hotel entrance, and three drivers, looking for a fare, quickly approached us. I showed the address to the first driver. He shook his head

Lines wait to visit St. Basil's Cathedral, while black market taxis operate around the corner.

and walked away. The second man said, "Nyet" and did likewise. The third driver looked at the address. He waited until the other two were out of earshot, then said in English, "I'll take you there for ten American dollars."

I said okay and we piled into the cab. To our surprise, it wasn't really a cab. At least, it had no meter. As we pulled away, I had a fleeting vision of seeing Siberia long before our scheduled visit, but decided I'd been seeing too many cloak-and-dagger spy dramas on television at home.

We saw a lot of Moscow on the way to the Yakirs' apartment in a suburban area. The huge city seems to stretch on forever. We arrived at a large apartment complex and drove in. Our driver hadn't spoken a word to us since we struck the deal. He stopped and asked several bystanders for directions to the building we were seeking and finally found someone who could help him.

As we pulled up before the building, the driver pointed and said, "Top floor." I asked him to wait. Shirley waited too as I climbed five flights of stairs to find out if anybody was home. There were only two apartments on the floor. I knocked at the door of the apartment on the right. Almost at once, a man answered from behind the closed door, "Who is it?"

"Is this the Yakir residence?" I asked.

"Yes."

I introduced myself.

"Will you please wait a minute?" The tone was pleasant. "I've been resting and have to put on some clothes. I'll be right there."

"Don't rush," I responded. "I'm going back downstairs to pay the cab driver and get my wife."

Evgeny Yakir was standing in the open doorway when we returned. A fine-looking man of medium height, he smiled. "Welcome to Moscow," he said in excellent English.

Evgeny escorted us into his small study which doubled as a bedroom. Behind his desk were stacks of books. We

Black Market Hack Gets a Ransom for a Ride

exchanged a few pleasantries. I told him about the taxi driver who had demanded American money.

Evgeny laughed. That's not unusual. The black market flourishes in Moscow. Did you have rubles with you?"

"Yes. I cashed them at the bank next to the hotel. They gave me seventy-eight rubles for a hundred dollars."

Evgeny said, "Do you have any idea how many rubles a hundred American dollars buys on the street? Four hundred, maybe five. The ten dollars you just gave that driver are worth forty or fifty rubles to him. Of course, you could get into deep trouble dealing with black marketeers."

"Don't worry," I hastened to assure him. "I wouldn't touch those fellows with a ten-foot pole. They were all over us on the streets of Leningrad. Wanting to trade rubles for dollars, and even trying to buy any clothing we were willing to sell them, I guess so they could turn around and sell it for a big profit on the black market."

Evgeny nodded. Just then we heard a knock at the door. Evgeny returned with our cab driver. In our excitement, we had left Shirley's Nikon camera in his car. The man told Evgeny in Russian that he expected a tip for his honesty and would like American money.

Evgeny shook his head. I rewarded the driver in rubles and he left disappointed.

CHAPTER 19

"TWELVE YEARS IS LONG ENOUGH TO WAIT..."

EVGENY INVITED US to sit down and said he would put on a pot of tea. He apologized for the fact that Rimma, his wife, was at work. "She would have been so happy to meet you," he said.

As Shirley and I sipped the tea, Evgeny talked about the 12 long years his family had been waiting for permission to leave the Soviet Union and emigrate to Israel. In 1973, when he, Rimma, and their son, Alexandr, then 18 years old, mutually agreed to seek visas, Evgeny had been a professor of mechanical engineering at Moscow University. He also headed an industrial plant. Rimma was a computer scientist, he said, and Alexandr was working toward his master's equivalency in electrical engineering at a Moscow institute.

"We had everything then. That year, before we decided to make the move, we bought this apartment — condominium, as you would call it. It was ours, the three of us. We didn't have to share it with another family," Evgeny said proudly. It was tiny ... that room where he spent so

"Twelve Years Is Long Enough to Wait..."

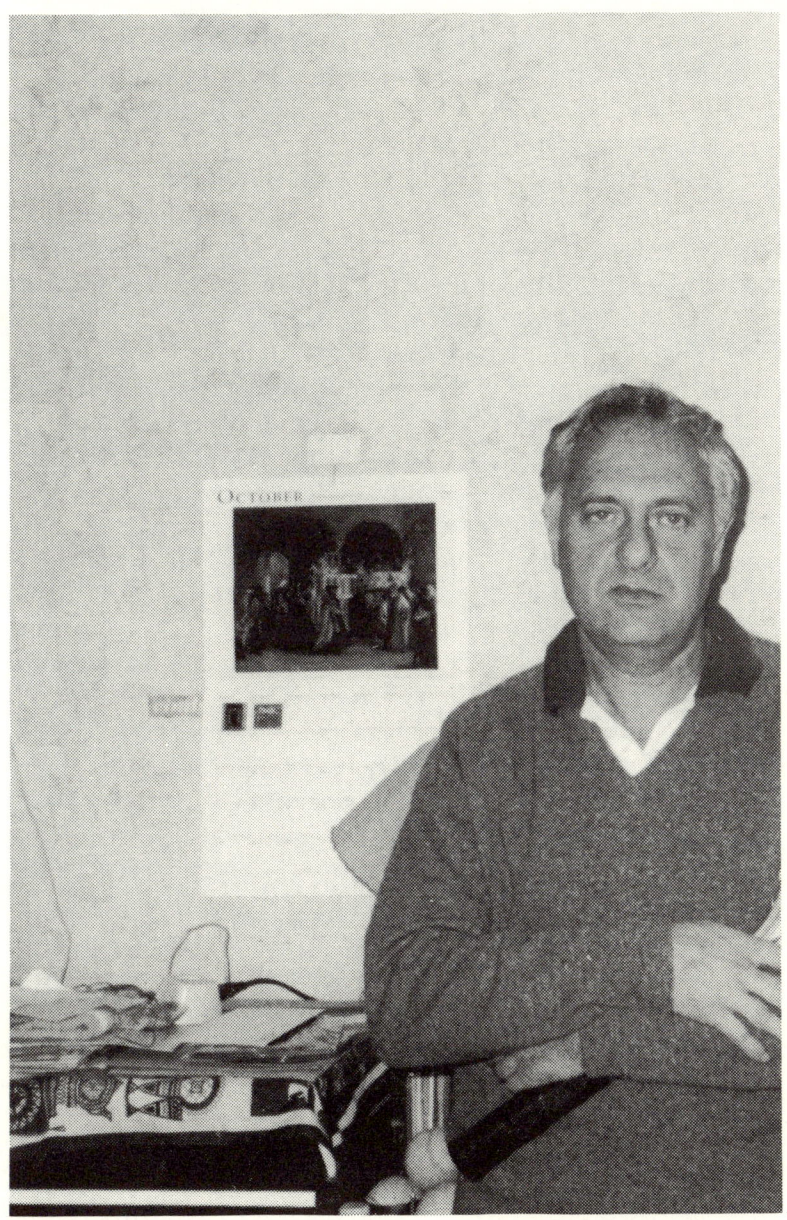

Evgeny Yakir, Soviet Refusenik.

much of his time, a kitchen and bathroom with less space combined than a closet in many American apartments, and another small bedroom that had been Alexandr's.

The little room in which we talked was indeed an all-purpose room. It contained Evgeny's books, desk, a bed, a dinette set, and a radio that sat on a small table. The entire "condominium" occupied an area of about 300 square feet, roughly the size of a small "single" apartment in the U.S., or a moderate-sized dining room in a middle-class American home.

While the Yakirs had been fortunate in their former position to buy their apartment, located on the outskirts of Moscow, and to escape sharing a rental unit, they still did not escape the clutter that comes with too little space and inadequate closet and storage facilities.

To encourage Soviet citizens today to purchase their own apartments, the government offers a one-percent-interest purchase plan that still requires a relatively sizable down payment. Those without the cash continue to rent and to share facilities that never seem to catch up with the housing shortage.

"Our applications were refused, so we became *Refuseniks*, a word originated here in Russia," Evgeny went on. "We applied again and again. After my first request, I was removed from my position at the university. Rimma lost her job too."

Although Rimma works as a custodian at a tennis club, Evgeny has no regular employment. For a time, he served as a scientific translator, but the government powers that be even stopped that. And Alexandr...?

"It's a sad story," Evgeny said as he sat facing our video camera. "Our son first applied for his visa with us. Then, he made several attempts on his own to get a visa for himself. He was continually refused. Despite his requests, he was allowed to continue his education, and he was graduated from the institute.

"But he had no chance to work at his profession after

graduation. Our son tried many different jobs and his last job was very funny. I believe Mr. Reagan had the same sort of job when he was young. Alexandr — Sasha, we call him — was a lifeguard."

Evgeny went on, "In June of 1984, Sasha was arrested, charged and sentenced for draft evasion, and now he is serving a two-year term in a — the Russians don't like to call it a labor camp, so they say it's a *correction colony*.

"Our son was 29 then and the upper limit for the draft is 27 in Russia. So when they arrested him, my attorney asked at the trial why they had waited until he no longer had the option of going to prison or to the army.

"They said they couldn't find him. He was living right here in this apartment. They couldn't find a person living in Moscow who was working for the police as a scuba diver fishing drunks out of the Moscow River?" Evgeny said incredulously.

Despite his bitterness concerning the treatment of his son, Evgeny was in an optimistic mood that day. He and Rimma would be visiting Alexandr within a few weeks to observe the young man's 30th birthday. And besides, he was optimistic about the new leader, Mikhail Gorbachev, who was then in Paris.

"The last administration was simply too old to do anything," he said. "They were just physically too tired. Gorbachev is very promising. He definitely has some ideas about improving the situation in Russia. He really, I believe, wants to start again the detente business, and if so I believe he will first have to solve the human rights question.

"It's been a long struggle. We still don't know what is going to happen to us. We always mean it when, year after year, we say, 'Next year in Jerusalem.' Many of our friends who have been successful in getting exit visas are unable to speak Russian anymore. Some who still know it, speak it with a Hebrew accent," he said with a wry smile.

Evgeny and Rimma did not know at the time of our visit

that on Alexandr's 30th birthday, Russian officials would give him the news that he would never be allowed to leave the country. He was told, we learned after our return, that if he shaped up and decided to become a good Russian he might at last be permitted to work in the profession for which he had studied. If he did not, the best he could hope for was a future doing odd jobs.

Those who know the Yakirs speculate that if they had been ordinary citizens, they might have been allowed to leave Russia when they first applied for an exit visa in 1973. Being highly educated and capable and coming from a well-known family (Evgeny's father was a colonel, his grandfather a general in the Russian army), their departure might have been interpreted as a slap in the face to the Soviet Union, another in a series of embarrassments, to a highly sensitive leadership.

Yakir continued optimistically, "The Russians use the excuse that those who had access to secret information would have to wait. We have waited. We don't know any secrets. Twelve years is long enough."

CHAPTER 20

IF BEARS CAN PLAY ICE HOCKEY...

Y OU AREN'T GOING to believe this anyway, so I might as well put the words to music and let you hum away your doubts.

HERE'S TO THE BEARS
(Sing to the tune of *The Daring Young Man on the Flying Trapeze*)
    Oh, they skated on ice with the greatest of ease.
    Those bold hockey players were bears, if you please.
    Their skill was so artful, applause wouldn't cease.
    At the circus in Moscow that day.
    Like hockey by humans they fought for the puck,
    Their goal shots were deadly, they didn't need luck.
    When roughness was called, they would head for the
      box.
    They were gentle-bears down to their socks.
    To those plucky bruins our glasses we raise.
    Bears playing hockey should be our new craze.
    This hilarious sight should make tensions decrease,
    And the Cold War to melt into peace!

I swear it, so help me. Drinking is not allowed at circuses in Russia, so we weren't seeing things. We actually witnessed an ice hockey game played by teams of four-legged bears. Black Russian bears in uniforms. Big ones. Which team won? The bears, of course. What was the score? Four to three. Or was it three to two? With all that excitement who can remember everything?

I've seen circuses before, but they don't hold a candle to a Moscow circus. Circuses abound all over the Soviet Union and even in independent Mongolia, which isn't really so independent because the country is occupied by the Soviet army. We saw a circus in Mongolia, but it didn't have a single ice-skating, hockey-playing contest featuring bears. But the People's Republic of Mongolia is just an emerging nation.

During our journey, we attended two circuses, three operas, one basketball game, and one hockey game played by humans, but nothing compared for entertainment with the bears except those two enchanting evenings on the Trans-Siberian Railroad. Seeing the famous Italian opera, *Rigoletto,* sung in Russian is an experience, though.

I'd like to show you the evidence because we shelled out about sixty rubles (80 American dollars) for video tapes of the Moscow Circus and the Bolshoi Ballet, both guaranteed to play on American VHS video recorders. The picture and music are as scrambled as a shortwave message sent to Russia by the Voice of America.

And who wants to stand behind the guarantee?

But I'm not mad. Seeing those bears was worth the price of admission, as well as the price of the tapes. When I think of the genius that went into training those bears to play ice hockey and show the winning spirit, I have hope for the Russian people.

FACES AND PLACES ...

Uniformed Young Pioneers are seen everywhere.

Faces and Places

GUM's department store, Red Square, Moscow.

A priest in the Soviet Union has doubts about the future of his city's only parish.

Faces and Places

Babushkas wait for mass to start.

Workers in the market in Tashkent, near the border of Afghanistan. The woman on the left is waiting to present flowers to Shirley in thanks for the Polaroid picture.

Faces and Places

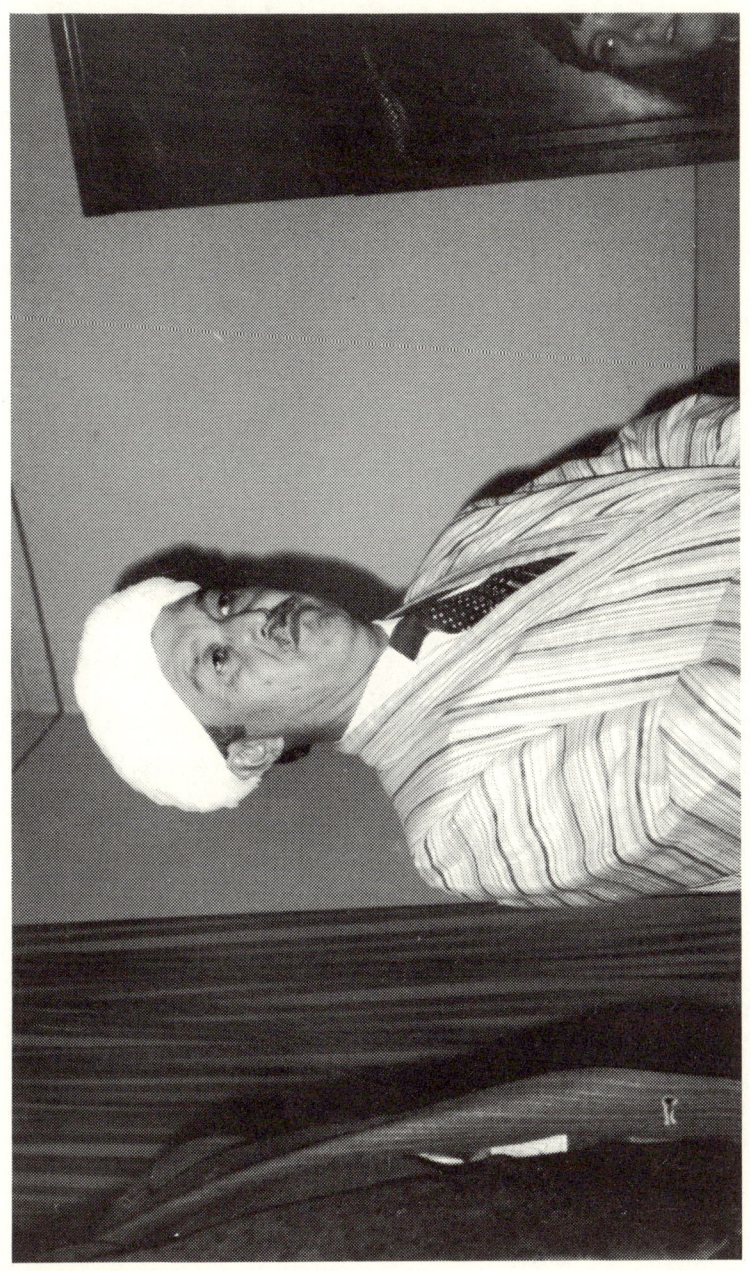

The leader of the Moslem community in Tashkent.

Nadia, our principal guide, interprets for us.

CHAPTER 21

IF I COULD HAVE ERASED NADIA'S FEARS

I GUESS NADIA, our official guide and interpreter, is conducting another group of Americans somewhere in the vast Soviet Union. I doubt that she'll have as interesting and exciting a group as ours because Nadia told Shirley and me in a farewell interview recorded by my TV camera that we were all very special.

"Every one of you is a chief. Not one is an Indian," Nadia said with a twinkle in her eye. And, of course, we were convinced that our highly educated, articulate main national Intourist guide wouldn't fib to us for one split moment. "You have been a real challenge for me. I have very much enjoyed our month together."

If we'd compiled a list of unforgettable persons we met on our trip across Russia, Nadia would have to be somewhere at the top. In many ways, Nadia was knowledgeable beyond her 32 or 33 years ("I'm over 30," she would say when questioned about her age).

She was a private person who respected our privacy, and although she had declared from the day we met her in Leningrad that she was dedicated to becoming a full-fledged member of the elite Communist Party someday, she never tried to force her "isms" down our throats. Some Communists were blatant in their attempts to convert us to their way of thinking.

There were times when she sided with us against the bureaucracy. Because most members of our group had traveled in many countries on every continent, we had experienced problems with so-called film-safe security equipment at airports, often losing irreplaceable film and shortening the normal life of our camera batteries.

At the Moscow airport on the way to Kiev at the beginning of our long series of flights, we decided to challenge the chief customs officer, a woman in uniform who could have fit in easily as a fullback for the Chicago Bears.

We asked her to hand-inspect the camera bags that contained our film and batteries. She refused, even after Nadia patiently interpreted our request. Such requests had never been turned down in other countries in recent years.

But the customs officer was not about to budge. She repeated the only English she apparently knew, "film safe," and again motioned to me to put our camera equipment through the detecting machine. I balked again, and Nadia continued to argue my case even though it was obvious she was getting nowhere with the woman bureaucrat.

The line behind us grew larger and noisier as some impatiently urged us to give in to the security officer's demands. But we held our ground. It was lose now and lose forever as far as I was concerned.

Finally, Shirley broke the deadlock and walked through the security gate. She came alongside the security officer, and I handed her my film, video cassettes and batteries. The security officer glowered as she saw what I had done but said nothing.

Then I put the empty camera into the carrying case and

If I Could Have Erased Nadia's Fears 97

sent it through the x-ray machine. Shirley retrieved the case as I walked through security. It was an unofficial SALT agreement with both sides saving face and declaring victory. But we had set a precedent for Nadia, and most of the time after that incident she helped us avoid showdowns. As a result, we managed to protect our film and the life of our batteries.

With all of her cool efficiency, Nadia had a hang-up that drew her close to most of us. She was so certain a nuclear war was coming that she and her husband, an assistant professor at Leningrad University, agreed they wouldn't have children. Nadia's fears had been compounded by the strong influence of her father, a disabled war veteran, who had instilled those fears in her since childhood. She mentioned them only once or twice, but the news became a matter of concern to all of us.

Along with a few others in our group, we took it upon ourselves to try to calm Nadia's concerns. Unfortunately, I didn't have my magic eraser that worked so well when my children were little and would wake up from a bad dream.

Nadia, the woman, had to live daily with a little girl's nightmare.

Shirley's woman-to-woman assurances were probably more effective. All I could do was repeat, "Nadia, please tell your father for me not to worry about peace, that I meant what I said. There will never be a war between the United States and the Soviet Union."

The well-intentioned words of an American traveler may be long forgotten by now, but I somehow believe that Nadia's response betrayed a glimmer of optimism when she said, "I hope that somehow we can reach an agreement. Your people are a great nation. Our people set many good examples to follow. . . ."

I don't remember what Nadia said next. But as we said goodbye to her in Irkutsk, Siberia, we were convinced that Nadia represented the best of Russia and the real hope for its future.

CHAPTER 22

BEWARE OF FRIENDSHIP TOURS

SEVERAL TIMES we've been asked if we would like to go back to Russia sometime. Without hesitating, Shirley and I have answered, "Never."

We've never said never about any other country we've visited. Each one has been better than we expected: India, except for the big cities like Bombay, is cleaner; China, friendlier; Romania, freer; Egypt and Syria, more intriguing.

But there's only one country like the Soviet Union — also referred to in this book as Russia, the USSR and a few other things. The darned bureaucracy wouldn't let us like it. Every time we thought we were going to, the red tape and petty harassment would shake us back to cold reality. Those bureaucrats don't want us to like them, they want us to fear them just as their people do.

And unless we learn to understand the game of Russian roulette they are playing with us, the peace between our nations that's certain to come someday will remain elusive. For now, there's a glimmer of hope that President Reagan and Secretary General Gorbachev understand what makes each other tick; such understanding is a

Beware of Friendship Tours

prerequisite for meaningful agreement.

I would never suggest to any American that he skip a trip to Russia. Everyone should see it for himself and form his own opinions. And I suggest he go there between June 1 and November 1, because the best part, beautiful Siberia, is no place for a tourist the rest of the year. Brrrr.

But traveler, beware. Don't get caught in one of Russia's propaganda nets. The government is subsidizing a great many Friendship tours and promoting them through questionable travel agencies in the United States. In Odessa, we met a fellow from California who bragged to us that he was getting rich booking those Friendship tours — mostly made up of women from the West Coast. He was personally escorting a couple of busloads of enthusiastic ladies and wanted to buy us a drink to tell us more about his profitable promotion.

We'd already been tipped off about the Friendship tours by the American Embassy and a few other reliable sources, who described them as made to order for Soviets who are experts in distorting facts. Take the housing shortage, as one example, they said. For more than 30 years, it's been a primary excuse for the country's low standard of living.

But the latest gimmick of the Friendship tours is to pretend that most ordinary Russians no longer live in tiny, cramped apartments, often shared by two families. Eager, peace-loving, gullible tourists are shown spacious, airy model apartments, the kind average Americans would be proud to call home.

The catch is that these apartments are reserved for the privileged classes in the world's most class-conscious social system. Meanwhile, young couples marry and are dependent on living with their parents for at least three years before they are eligible to get their own apartments. Because Russia needs people to inhabit developing regions of the vast country, newlyweds are informed that it's their patriotic duty to have as many children as possible as quickly as possible.

Stifled by the crowded conditions, their tempers flaring, they head for the bars instead.

The greedy American travel agent takes a hand in the charade, not giving a hang that the Americans he's escorting can't wait to get back home to spread the phony gospel of Russia's "progress" and Russia's outstretched hand of friendship.

How much misunderstanding and confusion are these good ladies spreading? Plenty. Their wishful thinking is only interpreted by the Kremlin as softhearted sentiment.

And the travel agent from California wondered why we wouldn't have a drink with him.

CHAPTER 23

EVERYONE BUT THE PUBLIC HAS A RIGHT TO KNOW

KONSTANTIN APOSHANSKY, Tass correspondent of the Crimea, greeted us with a broad smile as he met our plane at Simferopol, a busy town just a couple of hours by bus from the resort city, Yalta.

Although he knew no English, Aposhansky told us through our interpreter, Nadia, that he was pleased to arrange a panel discussion in Yalta for our group. He added with an attempt at humor that he'd been informed we were a little bored with sightseeing and wanted more of an exchange of ideas with Soviet citizens.

Later that afternoon, we met after a brief visit to the former palace of Czar Nicholas, where in February 1945, an ailing F.D.R. signed the Yalta agreement that gave away the store to Premier Joseph Stalin.

Some of us were late getting to the second floor of the brand new Yalta Hotel, an imposing 1,250-room stone and marble structure overlooking the scenic Black Sea. It was a long climb to the 14th floor and down again. As usual, the elevators were acting up as they do all over the Soviet

Union, and after waiting in vain for a ride, we relied on our legs.

Three Soviet professors were seated at the end of a long conference table and it was soon obvious that Dr. Edward A. Ivanian, chairman of the history section at the Moscow Institute of United States and Canada Studies, was running the show. After informing us that the United States and Soviet Union were at "the most difficult period of our relations in history" and chastising us for permitting our editorial cartoonists to ridicule Soviet leaders, Ivanian opened the meeting to questions from our group.

A publisher wanted to know how the Soviets could justify shooting down a Korean passenger plane (Flight 007) and killing its passengers.

Ivanian was waiting for that one. "Remember the Eisenhower U-2 incident? He had to apologize to us for that. Take my word for it. In a year or so you will know the truth about that Korean plane."

"You claim it was a spy plane, sir. Even if you believed that, did it warrant the murder of 269 persons? They all couldn't have been spies...."

"You wait until the real story comes out. Next question."

"Most of the world's newspapers are filled with stories about plane crashes. In the Soviet press we seldom see a reference to any plane accident occurring on your soil or a wire service release from Moscow concerning one. Don't you have plane crashes?"

Dr. Ivanian responded, "Yes, we do, occasionally. But our policy is different from yours. We believe the Soviet people do not need to know bad news. If there are injuries or deaths resulting from a plane crash, we notify the next of kin. That's enough. We don't have to put it in the paper."

And Afghanistan? Dr. Ivanian apparently hadn't heard the latest Soviet sentiment about having to get out of there. Dr. Ivanian heatedly justified the Russian invasion and

Everyone But the Public Has a Right to Know

Stalin and FDR at Yalta.

predicted a Soviet victory in Afghanistan soon.

That evening at a dinner in our honor, the other two professors on the panel joined us. When we asked them about Dr. Ivanian's absence, Dr. Dubrovsky, an English professor, replied, "We have never seen him before. He is from Moscow; we are from the university 60 miles from here."

"Is Dr. Ivanian a spokesman for the Communist Party?" we asked. Both doctors said they were fairly certain he was. They said *they* were not Communists.

Konstantin Aposhansky of Tass hadn't stayed for dinner, but he had done his job well for his Soviet state news agency. He had brought in a ringer from Moscow to bait us, badger us, bully and belittle us. In the end, however, Dr. Edward A. Ivanian, as hard-lined a Communist spokesman as we encountered in all of the Soviet Union, blew his cool.

Luckily for us, we kept ours.

CHAPTER 24

DR. VOLCHENKO RAPS OPEN-HEART SURGERY

DR. VOLCHENKO commented that open-heart surgery was a rarity in the Soviet Union because "Our medical profession doesn't believe in it. We can accomplish the same thing with medicine."

At the dinner table in Yalta — a special banquet arranged for us by Tass, the official Soviet news agency — I commented to the professor that I'd had open-heart surgery in 1977 and was feeling fine. "Five bypasses for the price of one," I joked.

Dr. Volchenko didn't get the humor. "Such surgery is terribly expensive. How did you manage to pay the bills? They must have cost thousands of dollars."

"Many thousands," I replied. "But the surgery is commonplace in the United States. At our company, we have basic health insurance and major medical for all of our employees and the company pays for it. Even an operation as expensive as mine is almost completely

The author with the chief of staff in a large hospital in Khabarovsk.

covered by our policies. All over America, people have such policies, either paid for by their companies or by themselves."

Dr. Volchenko was incredulous. "I can't believe that. I'm sorry."

"Well, it's true of course," Shirley chimed in. "If you don't believe us, just ask anyone at our table." That's exactly what Dr. Volchenko did. The distinguished professor of medicine not only asked anyone, he asked everyone.

And everyone at our table assured him that we had told the truth.

"Such a policy would bankrupt us," he said. "We have free medical care for everyone, but it doesn't allow for such costly operations as that. Besides, we don't need them; we can treat our patients medically and get equally good results."

Dr. Volchenko was rationalizing, and we knew it. We discovered later that he had approached us and asked to sit with us because he'd been briefed that Shirley was a state director of the American Cancer Society and that I was a member of the Advisory Council of the University of Kansas Medical Center. Such information was known to our national guides and passed along to the Tass correspondent.

A couple of weeks later, we visited a large hospital in Khabarovsk, which serves more than 1,000 patients at a time in several buildings on a campuslike site. We learned there that the hospital is just beginning to perform open-heart surgery and that in 1985 about three or four such cases were handled.

The chief of the medical staff at the hospital proudly showed us the wide range of equipment used to monitor and treat patients. American doctors, who return from Russian hospital visits, usually to the more sophisticated cities such as Moscow and Leningrad, say that medical facilities there are at least 20 to 25 years behind the United

States. And from my observations of the facilities at Khabarovsk I would say they were years behind Moscow and Leningrad.

The world's No. 2 superpower has a long way to go to catch up with the United States, Japan, Western Europe and much of the rest of the world in the field of medicine and medical research, as in most other fields of 20th century discovery and development.

CHAPTER 25

KIDS TAKE OUR WORDS WITH A GRAIN OF SALT

IN THE HEART of Siberia, an indescribably huge region of the Soviet Union which some travel folders humorously describe as the "Wild, Wild East," 30,000 persons study, work and live in an educational-research complex called Science City. On the campus, modern buildings in great numbers are screened by beautiful trees of the Siberian taiga (forest) and contrast sharply with the century-old architecture of nearby Novosibirsk, the Soviet Union's fifth largest city.

At the campus one Sunday in mid-October, we visited a model high school where a limited number of students from all over Siberia are accepted on the basis of competitive tests in mathematics and physics. Boys and girls between the ages of 16 and 18 live in dormitories, attend classes and work at their own pace in what their principal described to us as inventive thinking relating to physics and math.

These talented youngsters, their principal proudly said as Nadia, our national guide, interpreted, are at the knowledge level of first-year university students in the Soviet Union or "any top American university."

We were pleased to learn that many of them had "voluntarily" agreed to give up their free time that Sunday afternoon to sit in a classroom and exchange questions with us. The lack of that sort of personal contact and the overabundance of museum visits on our schedule had brought numerous complaints from our group.

Some of us took seats beside the students. Shirley sat with a pretty girl from Kamchatka in the Russian Far East Territory. When she introduced herself and her young Russian companion to our group, I was reminded of the months during World War II when my battleship, the USS *Idaho*, patrolled the Aleutian Islands from Dutch Harbor, Alaska, to the boundary of the USSR's international waters. Only a sneeze beyond that boundary and those mysterious, icy waters lay the peninsula of Kamchatka.

What was uppermost on the minds of these handsome, freshly groomed young people that afternoon? Physics and math? Of course not. War and peace. At first, the students wanted to show off their English, which is taught to them in the high school, but the well-meaning idea didn't work.

Even these quick learners couldn't frame a simple question in English. We didn't blame them, of course. At their worst, they were better at their attempt to communicate in our language than any of us were in theirs. Besides, where and when were they going to use conversational English? On a scale of 1 to 10, their chances of talking with English-speaking people other than their teacher were not much better than zero.

After the first question was haltingly posed by a persistent young man, it was unanimously agreed that we would use the interpreters. "Was the United States really going to attack the Soviet Union — and were we going to have a nuclear war?" the boy asked.

"Of course not. America doesn't want war with Russia.

Kids Take Our Words with a Grain of Salt 111

America doesn't want war with anyone. A nuclear war between our two countries is absolutely unthinkable." Some of us took turns reassuring the youngsters.

To the credit of the principal, he made no effort to halt our efforts to counter the constant, fear-inspiring Soviet propaganda that prompted those questions. The message usually adds that while Americans aren't bad people, their leaders in Congress and the president are stooges of the arms makers.

Whether or not we eased any of those young minds, we'll never know. The students eventually turned to another topic, politics. Never having met American journalists, they were eager to know if our newspapers had to support the party in power or, inasmuch as we had a two-party system, how it was decided which party we could support.

They were skeptical when we assured them that we had the constitutionally guaranteed freedom to choose which party and which candidates we would support, if we cared to make endorsements.

Our assertions were just too much for these young people to swallow. It was one thing for them to be allowed to question mathematics and physics. Questioning the philosophy of a nation's political leadership, however, was unthinkable.

But we tried. And we were grateful for the opportunity that high school principal gave us to speak our piece.

CHAPTER 26

SOVIET CUSTOMS INSPECTORS MASTER ART OF HARASSMENT

A TRAIN RIDE FROM IRKUTSK, SIBERIA, to Ulan Bator, capital of the People's Republic of Mongolia, took more than 35 hours. The distance was less than 700 miles, but almost an entire day was lost while we waited at a Soviet railroad station near the Mongolian border for a new engine to replace the old one that had carried us more than halfway to our destination.

We killed time by eating a quick lunch inside the station, walking a couple of blocks in the chilly afternoon air and visiting the area's only souvenir shop several times to come in from the cold. The store offered a small selection of merchandise for rubles only. Everything was greatly overpriced in comparison to the items sold for foreign currency at the tourist Beriozkas, so our group made very few purchases at the store near the station.

When our car was finally hooked up to the new engine late that afternoon, we were allowed to board it. But another couple of hours elapsed as we awaited a customs inspection. We were confined to our compartments while a contingent of Russian soldiers went from one compartment to another examining notes, diaries, tape recorders, and even the literature we were reading.

Three soldiers entered our compartment, all wearing heavy coats. The leader, a youngish, sandy-haired officer, spoke in uncertain English. He asked first if we had any literature, notes or tape recordings in our possession that were unfavorable to the Soviet Union. We replied that we kept no notes and had no tape recorder. Our video camera, 35mm Nikon and Polaroid were in plain sight but he ignored them. Instead he asked to see the books we were reading. The first one he picked up was Lee Iacocca's autobiography.

"Who is this author?" he asked.

"The president of Chrysler," I replied.

"He's the president of the United States?" the officer asked, with a puzzled look.

"No. He is the president of an American motor car company."

The officer seemed satisfied after thumbing through the book quickly. Then he turned his attention to a book Shirley was reading. He picked it up and turned the pages.

"What is this?"

Shirley answered, "It's a mystery book. A thriller."

The officer tried to look stern. "Is this about Russia?"

Shirley assured him it wasn't. We had decided at home to leave the Russian spy stories on our library shelves. "It's just entertainment. I read these books to relax," she said.

The officer nodded and it seemed for a moment that he wanted to smile, but didn't. "Have a nice trip," he said abruptly, and left with his aides.

Although Ulan Bator (also spelled Ulaanbaatar) is a progressive-looking city of nearly half a million, our stay of only a day — cut short from a scheduled two days by the delays — is best remembered for two things: the estimated 40 divisions of Soviet troops that occupy the country as a result of a 1966 Mongolian-Soviet mutual assistance pact, and the world-famous cashmere sweaters sold in a Beriozka for about $40 in U.S. money. Modern buildings and high-rise apartments abound in the capital city, although a visit to a rural area by bus gave us occasional glimpses of rows of portable shacks mostly hidden from the highway by tall fences.

The train we rode to Mongolia originated in Moscow and after crossing the Gobi Desert continued all the way to Peking, China, Mongolia's neighbor to the south. We were grateful that we would be returning to Siberia by plane.

At the airport back in Irkutsk, after a flight of a little more than an hour, we endured a customs inspection that made the one on the train seem like a hospitality session. Not only was our luggage painstakingly examined, but for two solid hours customs officials went through our notes, books, film, tapes, and other possessions. A record album belonging to one of the couples in our group was confiscated with the curt explanation that the composer was no longer in favor with the Soviet government. It had been purchased in a Soviet-owned music store. A booklet of knitting instructions was seized by a suspicious inspector who must have concluded it contained a secret code for blowing up the Kremlin.

Before long, the customs inspectors had confiscated almost everything from personal items to cameras and film. Yet, miraculously, nobody even asked about our video camera. As noontime neared, our stomachs began to growl. We had left our Mongolian hotel too early for breakfast, and, as usual, no food was served on the plane. We insisted that our local guides demand that the customs officials stop the nonsense and let us get to our hotel. Every other passenger on the plane had long since cleared customs.

The chief inspector's response was, "Tell them to stop complaining. We don't treat our own people any better."

Soviet Customs Inspectors Master Art of Harassment

How we missed our national guide, Nadia, who had returned to Leningrad! Either the inspectors got hungry themselves or somebody received an official phone call, but almost precisely at 12 o'clock, we received orders to close up our suitcases and prepare to board the bus that had been waiting outside the terminal. Our baggage was loaded first and at the very last moment, every confiscated item was returned to its owners.

Off we went to lunch at our hotel, wondering what the paranoids were saying about us as they ate *their* lunch.

CHAPTER 27

INDEPENDENT SPIRITS ABOUND IN SIBERIA

THE WORD "RELAXED" would hardly apply anywhere in the Soviet Union, but let's say people in other parts of the country don't seem as tense as they do in Moscow. It was generally agreed among us that the farther we got from Moscow, the less restricted everyone seemed to feel. Even the air seemed lighter.

At a small hotel in a village near Lake Baikal in Siberia, we were headed for the dining room when we passed a bar that was open for business. Nadia, our national guide, was having a heated conversation with the bartender. They were speaking in Russian, of course, but an argument is an argument in any language.

A few customers seemed to be oblivious of the scene, but we couldn't wait to hear what Nadia had to tell us. When she came into the dining room, we were all ears.

"I was scolding him for selling liquor before 2 P.M.," she explained. "Everybody knows that Gorbachev has issued orders that forbid this. I told the bartender he could get himself into a lot of trouble for disobeying those orders.

Independent Spirits Abound in Siberia

Why, it was only 12 o'clock when he opened."

"What did he say, Nadia?" someone asked.

"The stupid man said to me, 'You must be thinking about Moscow and Leningrad. We don't pay any attention to those things in Siberia.'" Suddenly Nadia broke into laughter. It was obvious she didn't intend to report him. Considering that Nadia was bucking for an invitation to join the Communist Party, we thought it was very sporting of her not to play policewoman. The KGB gets around, and sooner or later one of the secret police would find out about this free spirit of the spirits department.

Whether they would crack down was another matter. Bartenders who go to Siberia of their own free will aren't that plentiful. Like other workers, however, they are paid extra for "hazardous or unpleasant duty"... 10 percent above government scale in Novosibirsk and 15 percent above in Irkutsk.

Lake Baikal is only 40 miles from Irkutsk, and buses run regularly. Deepest in the world among freshwater lakes (its depth is one mile), Baikal is a fisherman's paradise. The road from Irkutsk is kept open by snow plows all winter for ice fishing, and a bartender is usually kept busy thawing out frozen fishermen.

It's no wonder the fellow we saw was so independent. He didn't need to put up with any guff. He could move to the Arctic tundra and earn double the going pay scale if he wasn't appreciated at Lake Baikal. But he wouldn't have as much fun. At Baikal, which averages 2,000 earthquakes annually, a bartender can mix a frozen daiquiri without moving his hands.

For any of my readers who might be interested in other fringe benefits, persons who have worked 15 years in Siberia can retire with full benefits, men at 55 instead of 60 and women at 50 instead of 55.

"Come to Beautiful Siberia" posters are available at the hotel in Irkutsk for only two American dollars.

CHAPTER 28

A SURPRISING CROWD AT KIEV'S SYNAGOGUE

WE HADN'T MEANT to disrupt services at the synagogue in Kiev, but our entrance caused a stir of excitement. To our surprise, the sanctuary was more than half filled. When we left our hotel after making excuses to our national guides for not accompanying the group on another museum tour, we were gambling that we'd find someone at the synagogue that Sunday morning in early October.

Our visit could hardly have taken place at a better time for us. This was a holiday called Simhat Torah. From the platform *(bimah)*, a distinguished, white-haired man signaled to the congregation to quiet down; then, as the ritual chanting continued, he walked quickly to the back of the room to greet us.

In our broken-toothed Yiddish, we managed to communicate with the well-dressed, dignified president of the congregation, who appeared to be in his early 70s. After seeing that I was supplied with a yarmulka and prayer shawl and that Shirley had a traditional covering for her

A Surprising Crowd At Kiev's Synagogue

head, he escorted us to the front row, where we sat down on a long, high-backed bench.

The president returned to the *bimah* to lead the services but every now and then would turn his eyes from his prayer book to us and smile warmly. The sight of more than 200 Jews openly praying in the atheistic Soviet Union overwhelmed us. As we looked around, however, we noted that they were mostly elderly men.

The president joined us to ask if I would accept ritualistic honor *(aliyah)*, and if we would stay on to talk after services ended. We declined and told him we had broken the rules, so to speak, by leaving our group and that we would have to return to our hotel shortly.

He understood. Breaking his own rules, he chatted with us intermittently, answering the questions that we so eagerly asked. . . .

There are 260,000 Jews in Kiev. His figure was higher than estimates we'd seen in reference books. Most of them guessed about 180,000.

Did the government give them trouble for observing their religion?

A shrug. Only the young persons are bothered. If they show up, they get a quick visit from the authorities who remind them that religion will get them *nowhere* in Russia. So they almost never come. He looked around the small but beautiful old sanctuary at the faces in the crowd. "The years are going by. When we are gone, there won't be anybody to take our place."

The Communist Party elitists are counting on that.

I asked if I could take pictures of the services with my TV camera. He smiled. "You know it's against the rules. I'll ask the rabbi." He reported back that the rabbi said it's all right under the circumstances. "But please take the pictures from the back of the room."

I checked through my viewfinder. My video movies were going to come out fine. I'd be able to show them to groups back home.

Kiev's only synagogue.

A Surprising Crowd At Kiev's Synagogue

The president of the congregation leads a service with only the elderly in attendance.

An old woman sat alone in the last row. The section upstairs reserved for women was empty. I approached the woman and wished her a happy holiday. She began to cry and replied, "But I have nobody. My man and my son were killed in the war." I could have kicked myself for opening my big mouth.

The old men around me wanted to know where Shirley and I were from. When I said, "America," they nodded approvingly. It was time to go. We wished the president a year of good health and happiness.

Outside, we paused to take pictures of the handsome, ornate synagogue. Its name? The president had seemed surprised. What name? It's just the *Shul*.

A platoon of Russian soldiers marched down the quiet residential street and passed the building. We got a sudden chill and walked quickly in the opposite direction to find a taxi that would take us back to our hotel.

CHAPTER 29

HOW LONG BEFORE NOBODY COMES?

MORDECHAI LEVINSON is one of 8,000 Jews who live in Irkutsk, Siberia, a city of about a half million population. The sexton of the only functioning synagogue in town, Mordechai turned out to be one of the most pleasant persons we met on our entire trip. Similarly, Irkutsk, a bustling city that looks nothing like the bleak, colorless image of Siberia we'd carried in our minds, turned out to be the most pleasant and relaxed of all the Soviet communities we visited throughout the huge country.

Mordechai, a short, sprightly man of 70 and a bit on the plumpish side, was overjoyed to meet us, especially when he learned we could communicate with him through our limited ability to speak and understand Yiddish. With Zvi, his helper, a tall, bearded young man who appeared to have a slight learning disability, Mordechai insisted on showing us every detail of the plain, but immaculate, old synagogue that occupied the second floor of a 100-year-old brick building.

Although our visit was unexpected, Mordechai acted as if he were greeting long-lost relatives. To his delight, Shirley raved over the matzohs Mordechai and Zvi had made for the next Passover. They tasted so crisp, she said, as I photographed the three of them with my video camera. Beaming, Mordechai said, "We made them six months ago, Zvi and I." Zvi beamed too and demonstrated how the matzoh machine worked. To this journalist's mind, it looked like an ancient hand-fed printing press I'd learned to run in journalism school.

Standing on the *bimah* along with Mordechai and Zvi, I held the Torah that Zvi handed to me after opening the ark. Shirley stood in the empty sanctuary, taking movies as Mordechai answered the many questions on our minds.

The camera caught my enthusiasm and Mordechai's friendly response, but no photographic invention on earth could have captured my inner feelings at the moment. Were we really in a 19th century synagogue in the heart of Siberia — a synagogue that was not yet a museum? "Do many persons come here?" I asked Mordechai.

"On Yom Kippur a great many come. Five or six hundred. They are lined up outside. The rest of the year," he smiled, "it's different."

"Do you manage to get ten people on Saturday?" Mordechai looked surprised. "Not one *minyan* (quorum of ten), three or four." I wondered about the young people and said so.

Mordechai's answer came quickly. "No, the young people don't come. It's strictly the *alte* (the old)." Shirley and I both recalled the words of the synagogue president in Kiev. Whenever a young person attended services at a synagogue or church, he would immediately get a visit from a Communist spokesman who would remind him that the Soviet Union is an atheistic state and that his future would be jeopardized if he practiced his religion.

The only major exception to that policy is applied to Moslems who live in great numbers in Soviet Central

How Long Before Nobody Comes?

Asian republics near the borders of Afghanistan and Iran. They are allowed to follow their customs and religious beliefs. Even their refusal to let their sons serve in the Russian army against Afghanistan is tolerated by the Kremlin for the sake of domestic peace.

But this was Irkutsk, Siberia, 2,500 miles or more from Moscow. Yet, the long arm of the Kremlin kept a tight grip on its policy toward religion here, and Mordechai accepted this as a fact of life.

I changed the subject. "It's so cold here in Siberia. Soon it will get down to 50 below zero and stay that way until next May." Actually, we were two or three weeks away from the real winter freeze.

Mordechai laughed. "It's not as cold as it used to be. Many years ago, it really got cold." Three generations of hardy Siberian stock, along with an extra layer of tissue around his waistline, had inured him to the elements.

Shirley asked Mordechai if he would like to emigrate to Israel.

The question seemed to shock him. "What for? We live well here. They don't bother us. Many of our most important professors, scientists, advocates (lawyers) and doctors here are Jews. Gorbachev needles the Russians. He tells them in his speeches that one Jew can do what it takes three Russians to do," he added with a laugh.

It was obvious to us he meant what he said. What he had left out of his explanation, of course, was the fact that he and his fellow Jews were split into two groups. By far the larger group were the conformists — non-religious Jews who indeed were leaders or future leaders in science and technology and whom the Soviet Union would keep from becoming part of any "brain drain."

Mordechai belonged to the other group, the smaller one, whose lives still revolved around the little synagogue. So life was pleasant for them in the waning years. How long will it be until nobody comes and the upstairs will be rented out just as the main floor had been? Now a small factory and office facility, the entire ground floor once housed Hebrew classes for the youngsters of Irkutsk.

It was time to go. We followed Mordechai down the rickety stairs and went outside. Our taxi driver was patiently waiting. He still held in his hand the note I had handed him in front of our hotel. Written in Russian by an English-speaking clerk at the Service Bureau, it had simply said "Synagogue. Wait," per my instructions.

We said goodbye to Mordechai and to Zvi and the two stood waving to us as we drove off. Our cab driver, who was so different from the non-caring, sometimes black-marketing drivers we met in Moscow, had the meter on his taxi shut off during the 30 minutes or so that we were in the synagogue. As we passed through the downtown area and saw the public market, I motioned him to stop.

The fare on the meter was ridiculously low.

I tipped the driver generously. He shook my hand and said "spasibo." I said thanks to him in return.

CHAPTER 30

THIS REGION NEEDS A NAME CHANGE

SOME AMATEUR EXPLORER, digging around for remains of lost civilizations, might uncover better-known finds than the Jewish Autonomous Region of the Soviet Union. What? You've never heard of it? Join the crowd.

Our well-read group of newspaper publishers from all parts of the United States had never heard of it either. But there it was on the map the Soviet government had given us. Right on the route of the Trans-Siberian Railroad, only three hours away from our final stop, the city of Khabarovsk, in the Russian Far East Territory.

We were to pass through the vast region that borders the mighty Amur River that separated Siberia from China, and stop at the regional center — Birobidzhan! Another fantastic adventure. Alexi told us to be prepared to get up very early. We would be arriving at the station in Birobidzhan at daybreak.

I set the alarm, but woke up long before it was time for it to go off. At first it was too dark to see anything, but as I lay in my berth looking out the window, the sky began to brighten. Shirley awoke, and we dressed quickly. When we went out into the aisle, we found several companions already dressed, others waiting their turn to get into the washroom.

Dick and Maynard gave us the bad news. Alexi had just

Despite the glowing accounts of the so-called Jewish Autonomous Region depicted in this 1984 book, published by the Russian government, the entire area was off-limits to our group. Some Soviet officials concede that fewer than 10,000 Jewish people now inhabit the region.

This Region Needs a Name Change 129

told them we would not be permitted to get off the train at Birobidzhan. When it stopped, I ran to the platform of our car. The outside door was open, but there were no steps in place. I decided to jump to the ground, but a Russian army guard standing in the way gave me a gruff "Nyet!" I backed off and returned to our compartment. Shirley's face brightened in relief when she saw me.

The train station blocked our view from the window, but as we pulled away some minutes later, we caught glimpses of industrial buildings, little Siberian houses and an unusually large number of high-rise apartments. All became a blur as we picked up speed.

Birobidzhan was real even if we couldn't get off the train for a quick, closer look. At our hotel in Khabarovsk right after breakfast, I went to the Service Bureau and asked for a car and driver to take us back to Birobidzhan. We were spending two days in the city before taking off for Japan, so there ought to be plenty of time. . . .

The woman behind the desk looked at me as if I were crazy. "That's impossible. You couldn't go there without a visa, and it would take you at least two weeks to get one." A visa to go to a city that was part of the territory of Khabarovsk? I said that sounded awfully strange.

"The roads are bad."

"What about a plane?"

"No planes." She walked away.

At the newsstand in the lobby, I saw a handsome, hard-cover book filled with striking color pictures. On the cover, in English, were the words, "Jewish Autonomous Region." Below the title was the ever-present picture of Lenin. The title page inside revealed that the book had been printed in Moscow in 1984. Also inside was a pamphlet that served as a promotion for the book.

It began: "The Region's biography begins with the decision of the Central Executive Committee of the USSR, adopted on March 28, 1928, which says: 'Spare lands in the Amur River basin of the Far Eastern Territory, including the Birobidzhan region . . . shall be allotted to the working people of the Jewish nationality for their settlement needs. Before the Great October Socialist Revolution the Jews in Csarist Russia were one of the most deprived nationalities. . . .' " The pamphlet and book went on to describe in glowing terms the great success this experiment had encountered in the last 50 years.

I bought several copies to give to friends.

On the bus that day, Sonya, our local guide, referred to the many visits she and her family had made from Khabarovsk to Birobidzhan to see "the wonderful Yiddish plays there." Sometimes they would visit as often as two weekends a month, she said in excellent English.

"Great, but why can't we go there?" I asked.

"It's a long drive and the roads are bad."

The doors to Russia's alleged Shangri-La for the Jewish "nationality," *which is not a nationality but a religion*, were closed to us. Yet we knew the region was in business. Or had we seen a mirage? Here's how it is according to Webster: "Jewish Autonomous Region, also Birobidzhan, former autonomous region, E Soviet Russia, Asia, bordering on Amur River; area 14,085 sq. m.; pop. 108,000, dissolved 1952."

Whether or not the Jewish Autonomous Region exists, I may never know. But some active, perhaps thriving, industrial community is alive in that area, connected to civilization by the Trans-Siberian Railroad and some "bad roads" that I saw with my own eyes, if only through glass.

But if it does exist, it's certainly time for a change of name. "Thousands of Jews from the Ukraine, Byelorussia and elsewhere came out to visit their new homeland," the book says. That I'll buy. But I suspect they took a quick peek at the land whose soil can be planted only 75 to 90 days a year, because the temperature drops to 40 or 50 degrees below zero from November to May. And, I suspect most of them said, "This we need?" So they hopped the train and went back to where they came from.

CHAPTER 31

SHOW BIZ ON THE TRANS-SIBERIAN RAILROAD

TRAINS IN THE Soviet Union run on Moscow time, and that policy includes the famous Trans-Siberian Railroad, which crosses 11 time zones. The world's largest country could easily hold the United States, Western Europe and a big hunk of mainland China, with room to spare.

A special red hand on the clock outside the railroad stations kept everyone informed of the exact hour in Moscow. But a schedule of stops along our route to Khabarovsk in the Russian Far East Territory designating local times was posted in the aisle of our car. So far as we were concerned, that third hand was just a curiosity, another red symbol in a world of red symbols.

I'll say this for the Trans-Siberian Railroad. If, for example, a five-minute stop for loading and unloading passengers was indicated on our schedule, we could bet that in exactly five minutes the train would be rolling again. That certainty kept any of us from wandering too far and getting left behind.

A view from the Trans-Siberian Railroad.

Show Biz on the Trans-Siberian Railroad   133

The Orient Express it certainly wasn't. However, despite the mystique that surrounds the Trans-Siberian Railroad, nobody ever told us it was going to be another Orient Express. Oh, we did feel a little taken in at first because some of the Intourist travel promotions and tour books we'd read had brought visions of luxury to our minds. Visions such as bathrooms with real showers, clean linens for our berths, put on by female counterparts of the Pullman porter who once made American train travel such a delight. And, of course, plenty of clean towels.

Anything resembling those "as advertised luxuries" was a product of a practical joker's imagination. I'll take that back. A few special cars with those amenities are available for special occasions when diplomatic V.I.P.s or celebrities have occasion to travel. This time our train was free of such freeloaders.

Our car had two tiny, but smelly, toilets, one at each end, that obviously were in that condition so we wouldn't get homesick for our hotels. And each couple was given two hand towels to share for the journey. We didn't make a big deal of that because we were only going to be on the train three or four days.

A couple of resourceful gals in our group took over the toilet brigade and went to work with Lysol and paper towels in hand. The spray and the scrubbing helped, but the odor lingered on.

The men had better luck with their chores. We'd started a cooperative do-it-yourself brigade as soon as we discovered that the Russian railroad "unions" don't permit their baggage haulers to load luggage onto a train. There it was, standing on the platform next to our car, a month's load of luggage for 17 persons. We formed a line and got it all aboard and stored in luggage spaces at the top of our compartments. American ingenuity wasn't dead, just tired.

Our next order of business was to clean the outside windows. They had become so covered with dust during the Moscow to Irkutsk leg of the Trans-Siberian cross country run that we couldn't see through them. Somebody borrowed a ladder at the first stop and a couple of our eager beavers climbed up and cleaned those windows. Nobody from the railroad objected. That's a laugh. Unions in the Soviet Union don't work for the workers, they work for the government. And the government, for reasons it refused to share with us, doesn't want some things to work or some windows to be clean enough to see through.

The gals took their own chores in stride. Our hotel rooms had maid service. But the railroad workers didn't do beds, just as they didn't do windows, and didn't do baggage-loading.

A young woman in charge of our car definitely was not a Russian version of one of our oldtime Pullman porters.

She was a key lady, which I have a hunch put her in the class of a low-ranking secret agent. Not a KGB member, mind you, but, well, perhaps an understudy.

We never learned her name, because she stayed in her own little compartment most of the time with her boyfriend. We'd catch fleeting glances of her whenever the train would stop long enough for us to get off and walk around near the station. She would quickly lock each compartment door to safeguard our belongings and unlock it when we were back on board.

The girl's only other chores were to make some boiling water for tea, or our own instant coffee, early each morning and start the fire in our car's pot-bellied stove. She managed to keep the fire going strongest during the late evening hours and through the early part of the night, heating up our compartments to the point where some of us actually prayed for the 50 below zero temperatures that were still two or three weeks away.

At times, life on the train was like a game of chess in which our group of 17 tried to match wits with a girl of not much more than 17. We'd open the door at each end of our car, wedging them so they wouldn't close, and for a few

Show Biz on the Trans-Siberian Railroad 135

moments cool air would come in. Our adversary would quickly shut the doors and disappear into her compartment. We were no match for the key lady. I predict a long and successful future for her as a teacher of advanced courses in how to harass tourists.

On the other hand, if and when Mr. Gorbachev gets rid of some of the nonsense that's keeping his country so backward, our young adversary may be one of the first to join the ranks of the unemployed. I doubt that she would know how to put in a real day's work.

With the windows cleaned, we spent a lot of time looking at the changing scenery. At times, the Siberian landscape would resemble our plains and western states, at other times, the vast forests (taiga) would block our view for hours. When we passed through the wide open spaces, hills and low mountain ranges in the background framed a seemingly endless panorama of unspoiled beauty.

Most of the roughly 5,000 miles of railway from Moscow to Khabarovsk is now electrified, so only for a few stretches did our engines require diesel fuel. The train ran quietly, making only a few stops in the small number of villages and towns that separated civilization from the Wild, Wild East.

Typical hundred-year-old small wooden houses with their artistically painted shutters provided a romantic contrast to the sterile high rise government housing in the cities. The high rises were encroaching on the Siberian scene and were abundant in larger cities such as Novosibirsk and Irkutsk. Because of inside plumbing, they will inevitably replace the charming little landmarks so distinctively Siberian.

The minor discomforts I've described failed to dampen our excitement at just being on the Trans-Siberian. Even they were forgotten the first evening after dinner when the entertainment Alexi planned for us materialized. Our private dining car — private because the planners had arranged to separate the Russian tourists from our little group — was suddenly transformed into a night club. Stolid workers on the train suddenly came to life. They were in show business. A kitchen helper became a magician of the keys with his small accordion, and a powerfully built dishwasher, who it seemed could have crushed the whole kitchen with her hands, became a dainty ballerina whose feet hardly touched the floor. And we practiced singing a Russian folk song Alexi had taught us. Practiced until we made beautiful music together.

This was a night to remember, so I raced back to my compartment to get my video camera. When I showed a playback through the viewfinder to the dancing lady, she gave me a bear hug and rushed to get a small gift for me to show her appreciation. When Shirley gave her a Polaroid picture, the woman was overwhelmed and presented her with a gift too.

The squeeze-box (accordion) player at first brushed off my efforts to tip him for his musical contribution to one of our best evenings in Russia, but with a little coaxing he let me slip some rubles into the pocket of his jacket.

The next day, we passed the musician and the dancer on the way to breakfast. Neither seemed to remember us. Last night didn't exist. The daytime was reality. But we weren't upset. We were promised a second magical night of show business and we got it. Same time, same entertainers, same audience.

Too bad the Russian travelers weren't allowed to join in the fun. We tried to invite them but higher authority said, "Nyet."

All in all, the Trans-Siberian Railroad was a momentous experience. I can only add, despite my jabs about their "unions," that if Gorbachev can make the rest of his country run with the clockwork precision of the Trans-Siberian Railroad, he'll have it made.

CHAPTER 32

RUSSIA DIDN'T SCARE ME, THANKS TO MAX

BACK IN THE MIDDLE 1930s at the height of the Great Depression, I traveled by Greyhound bus to California to visit my father. He had been gone from the family for several years and, for most of that time, had lived with a Russian family. The head of the household was a tall, balding man in his late fifties. His name was Max.

My father was a quiet man. Max was loud. He would holler and threaten and scare everyone half to death. He always seemed mad, but I never saw him physically abuse his wife and children, or, for that matter, anyone.

I don't know why, but Max and I became friends. Maybe it was because he had never seen a kid who wasn't afraid of him. My father had arranged for room and board for me, and I learned to eat Russian cooking. I soon learned to like the meat and potatoes prepared by Max's hard-working wife, and to hate her cabbage borscht and terrible-tasting cooked grain called *kasha* which she made for almost every supper.

Max and I would have long talks, and I was flattered that

he treated me as if I had sense, when he insulted almost everyone else in sight. He and my father seldom spoke to each other. My father considered him a big fourflusher.

Yet, Max was president of just about every organization in the neighborhood. People would come to him for advice, and Max seemed to have an answer for every problem. I was intrigued by his self-confidence.

A man named Adolf Hitler was making loud noises in Germany and threatening to build a Nazi army that would raise Germany from the ashes of its World War I defeat. I asked Max about Hitler.

Max said Hitler was for real and that he was afraid of what the German dictator and his Nazi thugs might do to Europe. What would Russia do to stop Hitler? I wondered.

"Nothing," Max replied. "You notice how loud I talk? Do you know what a bluffer I am? That's the way we Russians act. Do you want to know the truth? One German soldier can lick two Russian soldiers with one hand tied behind his back. An American soldier needs both hands.

"I get what I want by bullying people. I scare the hell out of them and they feel like they're nothing, and I'm everything. Adolf Hitler does the same thing, but he's got the stomach to fight. The Russians have the stomach to talk big.

"I don't want to fight anybody. I ran away from Russia so I wouldn't have to serve in the army. I ran away from the czar for a second reason."

Max got up abruptly and walked out of the room. We never discussed the subject again.

I've carried the memory of his words for almost 50 years. They shook me like few words have shaken me since. I've thought of Max and spoken of him many times, and I can see his face now as he made that surprising confession.

I thought of Max many times on our journey through Russia, where I had the eerie sensation of seeing thousands of Maxes, from bureaucrats to store clerks, bullying, bluffing and generally scaring the hell out of the little people, tourists sometimes included. Shouting and rudeness come with the territory.

I thought of Max most when Sergei Chetverikov, at the Russian Foreign Ministry, switched from his blustering defense of the Afghanistan war and confessed that Russia had to get out, "But we don't know how." I had accidentally seen Max and Chet in rare moments of humility.

When people ask, after seeing our video films of the Soviet Union or reading my columns, "Weren't you afraid?" I simply answer no.

How I would like to add, "But I'll bet there are millions of quiet people in Russia who don't know what it's like *not* to be afraid."

I wasn't afraid because I remembered Max.

CHAPTER 33

COMFORTING THOUGHTS ON CHANCES FOR PEACE

IN IRKUTSK, SIBERIA, we were introduced to an American businessman who was attending a medical trade show at a hospital just a block or two from our hotel. Manufacturers of health-care equipment from West Germany and other western European countries, as well as the United States, were exhibiting the latest in medical machinery.

"The Russians are in need of upgrading a lot of the equipment they use in their hospitals," he said. "My firm would like to do business with them. The problem is they don't have hard currency. We can't accept their rubles because they aren't worth anything, and we're afraid they aren't a good credit risk even though they have natural resources they may be able to cash in for hard money.

"We'd like to help them get over the hump because they could become important customers," he added. "Right now, we're busy trying to figure out a way to do business, and the outlook isn't all together gloomy." He dropped a

Comforting Thoughts on Chances for Peace   141

hint that international politics might play a hand in helping the Soviet government bring the nation's hospitals up to worldwide modern standards.

With the Geneva summit then only a month away, we wondered whether Mr. Reagan and Mr. Gorbachev would get around to discussing the price of peace. Shirley and I recalled our experience in Egypt in 1975, more than two years before Anwar Sadat paid his surprise visit to Jerusalem to talk about peace with Israel. In Cairo, Sadat's minister of finance said to us, "We told our people Egypt won the 1973 war. Our young people said, 'Good! Now we won't have to fight any more. We have nothing to prove. Let us live and enjoy life like people do in other countries.'" He went on, "But Egypt is broke. Ninety-five percent of the proceeds from our annual cotton crops is pledged to Russia. We must pay for the arms she sold us to fight a war we know we didn't win." He told us candidly, "Sadat must get peace if he wants to remain in power."

The rest is history. Within the next four years, peace between Egypt and Israel was a reality. Sadat won the return of the Sinai, shared the Nobel Peace Prize with Menachem Begin, and, in exchange for signing the Camp David accords, received enough United States aid to put Egypt back on her feet.

Whether or not he ever settled the mortgage on his cotton crop we forgot to ask during our stay in the Soviet Union.

The Russians appear to be broke, too, but I seriously doubt that the people are restless. It would take a lot more in-depth study than we had time for to get a clue to that. But it appears the grownups are just as passive and obedient to supreme authority as the children and aren't about to put pressure on Gorbachev to do anything.

Yet, Mr. Gorbachev is making no bones about the fact that peace is essential if his economic goals are to be reached. The question is how much time does his accounting department give him to stall? And what will his price be to sign? I wouldn't for a moment imply that Soviet leader Gorbachev would ask Mr. Reagan to actually pay to sign an arms agreement.

But maybe Mr. Reagan has in mind something like loan credits or a solution to the problem of propping up Russia's worthless ruble. That shouldn't hurt Mr. Gorbachev's pride or create the impression that Russia can't continue going it alone, living like a third-rate, Third World power.

It's important that whatever he does, Ronald Reagan remains tough and aloof. The Russians get mighty nasty with people who talk nicely to them.

CHAPTER 34

A TRIBUTE TO RUSSIA'S ICE CREAM

WHAT'S GOOD to eat in Russia?
The caviar, of course. The bread, especially the black bread, anywhere it's baked. The cabbage borscht, if you happen to like cabbage. The roast beef, especially in the Ukraine where the well-fed cows die happy. The potatoes when they aren't served cold. The Chicken Kiev in Kiev.

Nobody starves in Russia, not even a spoiled American tourist.

But let me tell you what's great.

The ice cream.

Yes, the ice cream is so great that even though my doctor would have killed me for doing it, I sneaked a few spoonfuls almost every night even though I'm not supposed to eat it.

Russian ice cream should be the national symbol instead of the hammer and sickle, or the red star. It's much more soothing to the nerves.

Of all the things the Russians have to stand in line to get, I have to tell you the ice cream is indisputably worth it.

And do the Russians know it? Why else would they wait in line on a street corner in the bitter cold of Siberia just to buy an ice cream cone from a vendor?

I could tell you stories about Russian ice cream you wouldn't believe. Defectors have a change of heart and go back because they miss the ice cream. In Israel, Russian immigrants once threatened to go back to the salt mines if the quality of ice cream didn't improve. They won out and showed the Israelis how it should be made.

Today, Israel's ice cream ranks only behind Russia's as the best in the world.

Siberia wasn't frozen when we left it in late October. By November, I'm told, it is so bitterly cold that some of the vendors have to move in off the streets. If any of the hardy souls are still outdoors — after all, they have to be hardy to earn the 10 or 15 percent above pay scale they get for working in Siberia — I'll bet there's a line waiting to buy.

I won't miss the caviar. It's too rich for my blood. I won't even miss the delicious bread that much. Good bread we can always find at home, even if it isn't black. Russians can have the cabbage borscht. Our roast beef is better and our fried potatoes are just as cold. Chicken Kiev I can get anywhere.

But whenever I think of ice cream, I'll have a lump in my throat. It won't be indigestion. It will be one of the good things I'll remember about our trip to Russia.

CHAPTER 35

ALEXI IS AT A LOSS FOR WORDS

LIKE MANY young men in Russia, Alexi, our last national Intourist guide, was married when he was 18. The father of a four-year-old boy, Alexi, 26, spoke wistfully of the freedom from responsibility that hadn't been his to enjoy. He lamented that early marriages were responsible for Russia's high divorce rate.

But he wasn't bitter, and despite the fact that he would bait us from time to time with comments like, "You people are wealthy, but most Americans are standing in breadlines," or "There's so much gangsterism in America, everyone has to sleep with a gun under his pillow," none of us could dislike him.

Almost all of us took turns trying in vain to change his views.

Alexi had a goal that went beyond being just a tour guide. Like Nadia, whom he had relieved at Irkutsk so she could return to her home in Leningrad, Alexi wanted to become a member of the Communist Party. But unlike Nadia, he was preoccupied with talking and acting like a communist bureaucrat. Maybe it was because he felt so sure of his future.

Nadia was a woman in a society that only recently had recognized the importance of women. The loss of many millions of Russian men in World War II had forced the Kremlin to reevaluate things. With the shortage of men, women were permitted and encouraged to step in and fill the gap. Today, for example, there are more women than men serving as doctors. The ratio is about 60 percent to 40 percent.

Unfortunately for Nadia, she might more easily have succeeded in becoming a doctor than a member of the Communist Party, although at 32, she may yet achieve her goal. Doctors who aren't party members are not rated very highly in the stratified society. They make the equivalent of about 200 American dollars a month. Also, Nadia's father is a retired, disabled war veteran, who doesn't belong to the party and apparently does not wield much influence.

Alexi, on the other hand, believes he has a leg up on his ambition because his father is active in the party. An airline pilot, he is flying high on a salary about three times as great as that which a doctor commands.

While a heritage such as Alexi's isn't the final word, it certainly weighs heavily in the minds of the decision-makers who determine which of Russia's 280 million population will become part of the 18 to 20 million party elitists that run the country.

I think the turning point in our group's relationship with Alexi was late in coming because most of our words fell on deaf ears. But at Khabarovsk on one of the final evenings of our stay in the Soviet Union, we found ourselves with him at a time when he seemed most critical of our society.

Shirley, who was usually more patient than I, finally put her feelings into a few simple words. "Alexi," she said, "if you're happy with your way of life, wonderful, that's great. I'm happy with my way of life. I promise you I will

Alexi is at a Loss for Words

not impose my way of life on you, but don't ever try to impose your way of life on me."

It was as if the air suddenly whooshed out of Alexi's hot air balloon.

For once, this handsome boyish man seemed at a loss for words. If Shirley had angered him, he would have lashed back. He made no attempt to respond, but we knew her words had gotten through to him.

The night before we left for Japan, we threw a little party for Alexi. We presented him with a small gift we'd all chipped in to buy, raised our glasses of vodka and made a toast to health and to peace. Alexi was fighting back tears. He just didn't know how to accept such caring and concern from a bunch of Americans.

Alexi said his farewells. He wouldn't be seeing us the next morning, he said, because he had to return to Moscow on the 3 A.M. train and would be long gone before we were up. But the next morning, he was waiting for us when we came down to breakfast. He had received permission to take us to the airport and see us off.

For a few hours, at least, I would like to believe we left Alexi wondering if all the things he had been taught to believe were really true.

CHAPTER 36

HOW WE FINALLY GOT OUR COFFEE *WITH* BREAKFAST

It took a month and 10,000 miles of travel inside the Soviet Union to discover that Russia is spinning its wheels. It must start moving. The dreams and hopes of Vladimir Lenin, founder of the Communist Party, died when he died of a stroke in 1924, and nothing except the Russian war machine has worked since. Not the people, not the factories, not the farms, not the toilets, and certainly not the elevators.

Mikhail Gorbachev, who appears to have more finesse than his predecessors, is the most vocal critic of the worst system of organized inefficiency ever created by man. In another chapter, I have quoted some of the things he has to say about the weaknesses of the Soviet system even as he extols its virtues. Some of his own harsh words of criticism make my acid observations sound complimentary.

Now I must tell you what really makes me so sure that Ronald Reagan and Mikhail Gorbachev will open a new window — Reagan because he yearns to leave a significant arms agreement with Russia as his legacy, Gorbachev because he desperately must divert more of his nation's miserable GNP to increasing the Soviet standard of living.

The answer is coffee.

Yes, coffee. As trivial a matter as getting a cup of coffee with our breakfast gave me an insight into the bullying tactics that have given the Russians so much mileage around the globe for decades. In dining room after dining room, in city after city, region after region, including our favorite, Siberia, we complained, begged and pleaded for coffee with our breakfast. Always the coffee was served after breakfast.

This particular one of the inane customs and rules the Communists preserve by decree from Moscow was as unmovable as a mountain to seemingly intelligent and well-traveled newspaper people who put up with this frustration.

This form of the Russian torture system, administered by robotlike, unsmiling waiters and waitresses who knew darned well what we wanted, but ignored us, was tolerated not because we were afraid of the bullies. We kept thinking things would get better. They never did.

In Khabarovsk, a city in the Russian Far East bordering China's Manchuria which we could see across the wide Amur River, we decided to make a stand. Shirley and I barged into the dining room 15 minutes before it was scheduled to open. Shirley banged her fist on the table and said to the surprised waitress, "We want coffee now!" In an instant, the waitress returned with a trace of a smile, a pot of coffee and two cups. She invited us to sit down and even brought rolls and butter. Everyone in our group enjoyed hot coffee at breakfast that final morning in the Soviet Union.

If only we'd known how to handle bullies from the start, how much more tolerable those breakfasts would have been.

Mr. Reagan is an old hand at dealing with bullies. He and John Wayne did it for years. I can just see our leader smiling and saying between clenched teeth, "Mikhail Gorbachev, don't con me and I won't con you. Don't bully me and I won't bully you. We're here because we don't want to blow each other up. Now, let's get down to business. What'll it be? Coffee, tea or cocoa?"

Unless he's a fool, and I'm sure Mikhail Gorbachev is not, he will understand.

CHAPTER 37

NOW... A FEW WORDS FROM GORBACHEV

IF MY COMMENTS seem a trifle critical of the Soviet Union, get a load of what the boss man, Mikhail Gorbachev, has been saying.

I'm sure it wasn't by accident that a speech by Gorbachev to the Communist Party's elite Central Committee was lying in plain view on a small table when we arrived at our "private" waiting room at the Tashkent airport. I call it private because once again we were separated from the Russian tourists.

Because of a sudden and surprising October snowstorm in the normally warm city near the Afghanistan border, our plane to Siberia wouldn't be taking off for several hours. I'd like to think that some concerned Russian wanted to make sure we had something to read during our idle moments.

While a few members of our group worked off nervous energy by doing exercises, I devoured Gorbachev's words contained in a small pamphlet titled, "For the Forthcoming XXVIIth CPSU Congress. It was published in English by Novosti Press Agency Publishing House, Moscow 1985."

The following gave us a preview of what the Secretary General told the Central Committee and was scheduled to say to 5,000 delegates at the Communist Party's important 27th Congress, February 25, 1986:

*Executives in many ministries and enterprises try to get as much (from the state) as possible ... but their approach to rational utilization of resources is quite often irresponsible. Equipment sometimes stays idle or is not used to the full.

We must put an end to such waste immediately. It is obviously not enough to issue appeals only — there have been plenty of them. It is necessary more strictly to make persons answerable, legally answerable for their work.

*Good order must be established at every enterprise and construction site, at every collective and state farm, at every organization. Without this there can be no talk about any kind of rational economic management or the growth of the economy's efficiency.

In most sectors scientific and technological progress is taking place at a sluggish pace. ... There should be revolutionary changes. ... This means in fact a retooling of all the sectors of the national economy on the basis of up-to-date achievements of science and technology.

The goods produced fail to meet modern technological, economic, aesthetic, and, for that matter, all consumer requirements, and are sometimes of obviously inferior quality, which is actually plunder of material resources and waste of our people's labour effort.

*It is necessary to move forward more boldly along the path of broadening the rights of enterprises, their independence, of going over to the cost-accounting system and on this basis to increase the responsibility and interest of work collectives in the end results of their work.

Now ... A Few Words from Gorbachev

*It is time to start streamlining the organizational structures of management, to do away with unnecessary management, to simplify the apparatus and raise its efficiency.

*From the point of view of modern requirements, there should be a considerable improvement of the material and technical basis of the public health system, and the quality of medical services, and the population should be better supplied with medicines.

*There are quite a few other problems to which we should pay close attention and find the right solutions.

*These are an improvement of living conditions of young families; an improvement of mother-and-child care.

*And naturally, it is important ... to step up efforts aimed at solving such socially important problems as housing so that every family will soon be provided with a separate flat or house with all amenities.

*The rates of growth in labour productivity have slowed down. The situation with production, costs, profit and other indicators is not much better.

*Working people want to spend a greater part of their incomes on improving housing amenities, on leisure activities, on tours and excursions, etc. These requirements must be met more fully....

I brought the pamphlet home so that any time I might think I was too hard on the Soviet Union in my book, I could re-read Mikhail Gorbachev's candid words and also his critical comments printed in the Moscow News of September 29, 1985:

"This is a whole set of questions relating to economics, politics, morality. Low output quality is the bluntest case of squandering public funds as well as human work.

"One can understand the buyer who wonders why we know how to make spaceships and atomic-powered ships, but often produce defective household gadgets, shoes and clothes. And this involves not just financial, but also moral and political costs."

Now I'll let you in on another reason, Mr. Gorbachev, a most important one that seems to have escaped you. Management and labour may have their faults, but in Russia, as evidenced by eleven five-year plans that have flopped, the real culprit is The System. Tell that to the Central Committee of the Communist Party!

CHAPTER 38

WHERE COULD THEY SEND US—SIBERIA?

WHEN OUR press group entered Leningrad from Helsinki and Russian customs officials confiscated such forbidden items as our copies of *Newsweek* and *Time*, one inspector asked me, "What are you going to take with that TV camera?"

"Everything I'm allowed to take," I replied. In the weeks that followed, my TV camera and I were almost as conspicuous in the Soviet Union as the Red Star, Lenin's pictures and the Communist emblem, the hammer and sickle.

Nobody in authority ever commented to me again about the TV camera during our month-long visit that included Western Russia, Central Asian republics in the Soviet Union, Siberia, and the neighboring Soviet satellite country of Mongolia.

The camera was even ignored by customs officials during the harrowing two-hour inspection of all of our possessions at the airport in Irkutsk, Siberia, after our trip to Mongolia. One would think it would have appeared more sinister to the paranoid customs officials than the diagram for knitting, or the record album whose music had been composed by someone out of favor with the government, or our mystery novels and our notes, all of which were taken and later returned.

In our hotel room in Khabarovsk, many thousands of miles from Leningrad, on the night before our departure from the Soviet Union, I lay awake in my little bunklike bed thinking of the video cassettes with their hours of precious film footage I'd taken with my TV camera. My thoughts flashed back to that first customs inspector and his casual question, and I suddenly got the chilling feeling that all would not go well for us at the airport in the morning.

I recalled that about 10 years before, one of our reporters had gone to Moscow and Leningrad with a small group of newspaper people on an official mission sponsored by the Soviet government. Everyone took notes and pictures at the sessions and all of the notes and film were confiscated at the Moscow airport. Our reporter was a nervous wreck when she returned, and it seemed she would never forget that incident at the airport.

I made up my mind I was absolutely and positively going to resist any attempt to confiscate my video cassettes but didn't have the slightest idea how I'd go about it.

Early the following morning, I told Shirley of my fears. I wondered for a moment if she would think I was sounding like a paranoid tourist, but she took my concerns seriously. "What can we do?" she asked gamely.

"I think I have a plan. If necessary we will sacrifice one cassette, the last one we shot. It was only partially used. We'll date it from the time we entered the country in late September until today's date, October 25. I haven't recharged the batteries, they're dead, so I doubt they can find anything that can play back the one cassette. But if they want to take it anyway, I'll settle for that. The only

Where Could They Send Us—Siberia?

thing is, I haven't figured out what to do with the other cassettes."

Shirley had the answer. "I remember that whenever we were searched at customs, they never touched our bodies. We'll hide them on us." The conversation took place in our room, but we weren't concerned about it being overheard on some bugging device. Even the Soviet Union couldn't have enough agents to bug rooms in hotels 5,000 miles from Moscow. Or could it?

We stood in one of several lines at the airport waiting to go through customs. When it was our turn for inspection, Shirley handed our passports to an official. The man looked at them quickly and said, "Mr. Rose, I want to see your video camera and your video cassettes." I dragged our four pieces of heavy luggage and the camera carrying case into the small inspection area, unzipped the camera case and handed him the video camera. Shirley reached in her pocket and handed him the cassette we had decided to sacrifice.

The customs inspector looked at the lone cassette and said suspiciously, "Where are the others? Don't you have more cassettes?"

Shirley said calmly, "That's all we have."

He repeated the question to me. I replied, "There aren't any more."

The inspector called for his superior who came right over. The two conversed at length in Russian. At one point, the boss man held the cassette up to the light and tried to see inside it. He gave up the effort. After more conversation in Russian, he handed the cassette back to the customs inspector and disappeared.

The inspector asked us to open our bags and made a cursory examination of their contents. He then instructed us to close the bags, returned our passports, the video camera and the cassette and waved us through.

We found ourselves in a large, noisy waiting room where we would soon meet the others in our group and board our Soviet Aeroflot plane to Japan. Shirley and I breathed a sigh of relief. "Well, we made it," Shirley said. "And we've got *all* the cassettes on us. But it sure looked for a moment as if things were getting sticky."

I made a stab at humor, even though my stomach was still churning. "So what would they have done to us if they'd found the other cassettes — send us to Siberia? We're already there."

CHAPTER 39

RACING THOUGHTS ON THE BULLET TRAIN

THE FLIGHT FROM Khabarovsk to Nigata, Japan, took only a little over an hour.

When we arrived at the airport, Pat, our Japanese guide, said with a straight face, "Welcome to civilization."

"It's great to be home," we responded, and laughed at our goof.

All we needed was a Japanese band playing "The Star-Spangled Banner."

This had to be the first time Shirley and I had even halfway acknowledged that any foreign country could be called home. But we'd never spent a month in the Soviet Union before. We were still in a state of shock. Everything is relative, they say, and relatively speaking, Japan looked like Los Angeles West compared to what we'd just seen.

On the bullet train, speeding at 160 miles an hour to Tokyo that afternoon, I closed my eyes and saw Khabarovsk, a pleasant city of more than 500,000 population, that lags a half century behind Japan. I wondered how Khabarovsk residents would react if they could just visit the tiny neighboring island and see its miracles of modern technology.

"They wouldn't believe it," I said.

"The Russians? I know it," Shirley replied. "It's too bad Russia restricts its people so. They wouldn't have to see America to know what they're missing."

"There's more involved than just typical Russian repression," I added. "The ruble is worthless outside the country, and Russia couldn't supply the hard cash for travel even if the Kremlin eased up."

Shirley didn't answer. She was reading a paper — a real newspaper. We hadn't seen one since leaving Helsinki in September.

I thought about Khabarovsk again and of the times we'd stood on the bank of the wide Amur River and stared with fascination at China. Once Russia's faithful and obedient servant in the communist world, China went in search of new friends and found them. America was one.

China has turned her back on a losing proposition, Russian-style communism and is going Westward Ho at a pretty fast clip. We saw this coming when we visited that country six years ago. Then, Chinese officials predicted the country would begin a building boom with the help of foreign capital — "as soon as something can be done about the sewer system that dates back to the Ming Dynasty."

Neither those officials nor we dreamed that the sewer system could be modernized so fast. Now, Americans who want to build a hotel in China approach the government for permission and are told, "Where do you want to build it and how high would you like it?" Barring a change of heart by the still-communistic powers that be, China's alliance with America and other Western powers will catapult her into the 21st century far sooner than anyone believed possible six years ago.

If I were Mikhail Gorbachev, I'd hate to look across the Amur and contemplate what China is up to. Especially if I weren't sure that the Kremlin would support my plans to make Russia come alive.

But knowing I had only one chance to keep my country from going down the tube, I'd cozy up to President Reagan and tell him I'd gladly junk a pile of missiles if he'd agree to lend some hard cash and help modernize my own rotting sewer system.

Peace at that price would be a bargain for all of us.